Real Fresh Food

Real Fresh Food
HEALTHY MEALS FOR BUSY PEOPLE

ANNA & ROGER WILDE
WITH PHOTOGRAPHY BY DANIEL ALLEN

NH
NEW
HOLLAND

We dedicate this book to:

Our mothers, Kit and Marie, for encouraging us to cook from a young age, even when it meant cleaning up a big mess after we were finished.

The wonderful hardworking organic growers of Nelson who nourish our families – Wolfgang, Brent, Suzie and their teams.

The many teachers who inspired us over the years as we learned about food, natural health and happiness, including Holly Davis, Airdre Grant, Mareko Kasugai, Harada Tangen Roshi, Masao Kumagai, Glenn Dentice, Maggie Blake, Sonia Moriceau and Sharda Rogell.

Acknowledgements

The photography sessions were fun! Our profound thanks to Dan for being so relaxed and generous with his time and talent, also to Content kitchenware store in Nelson for supplying everything we needed to present our food beautifully. Thank you also to Jane for guidance with our writing.

We would also like to extend our gratitude to Gabriel's babysitters, especially Nana Ree, 'Aunty' Fran and Dodda, who provided us with many childfree hours for recipe-testing, photography and writing.

Contents

꧁❀❀❀❀❀❀❀❀❀❀꧂

Foreword

Real Fresh Food is a beautiful and timely book that will appeal to anyone with an interest in growing and cooking fresh, natural food that is good for you. This constitutes a large audience because, thankfully, more and more people are turning their backs on a modern, highly processed industrial diet and rediscovering the joys of growing, preparing and eating fresh, healthy food.

Roger and Anna Wilde teach us how to prepare and cook food so that it keeps its flavour, looks fantastic and retains its essential nutrients as well. Readers will be genuinely inspired by these sumptuous yet easy-to-prepare recipes and tips about how to eat for optimum health.

Roger and Anna's passion for fresh-tasting whole foods, a balanced diet and healthy living permeates this book, and I am certain that *Real Fresh Food* will introduce dozens of recipes that become firm favourites with the whole family.

Real Fresh Food is the perfect book for anyone interested in fresh food, great taste and healthy living.

SUE KEDGLEY

Sue Kedgley is a New Zealand Green Party MP and chairperson of the New Zealand Parliament Health Committee. She is also a founder of the Safe Food Campaign in New Zealand and the National Food Safety Network.

Introduction

We all want to be healthy and happy. Eating delicious, top-quality food is a great way to improve your life in so many ways.

Even with the best of intentions, the challenges and temptations of everyday life can lead to unhealthy eating habits. You may be living with constant stress, weight worries, exhaustion, digestive difficulties and emotional upheaval. Changing to a healthier way of eating might seem like yet another hassle to add to an already hectic lifestyle, but by putting diet-change into the too-hard basket, you may not realise the damage you are doing to your body.

A keen awareness of your body is the most valuable tool you have for managing your health; pain and discomfort are invitations to adjust behaviour. Learn to trust your intuition and experiment to discover which foods make you feel truly alive.

Believe it or not, you have the power to make hugely beneficial improvements to your health and happiness by introducing some simple changes to your diet. It's actually easier than you might realise to achieve and maintain a state of well-being, even amongst the complex challenges of modern life.

Despite common misconceptions, healthy food:
* is quick and easy to prepare;
* may be made from readily available ingredients;
* is delicious and interesting;
* can be enjoyable for the whole family, including doubtful kids;
* satisfies your cravings for sweets and special treats;
* is possible on any budget.

Try the recipes in this book and discover how delicious, economical and easy-to-prepare healthy food can be. A little experimentation with wholefoods will not only result in your feeling healthier and happier but will also introduce you to a whole new world of satisfying food.

Real Fresh Food calls for a return to healthy home cooking. Begin today by introducing gradual changes, incorporating our ideas into your daily routine as energy and time allow.

ANNA AND ROGER WILDE

Our recipe for healthy living

Preventative action based on diet, exercise and natural self-care is an effective way of looking after yourself and proper nutrition is just one aspect of that. Our recipe for healthy living includes 10 lifestyle factors additional to maintaining a healthy diet that offer opportunities for positive, effective action that will have an impact on your health.

1. GET MOVING

I used to avoid walking and any form of exercise. Gradually, I came to enjoy yoga and later got into hiking and biking. Now I like how exercise gives me a strong, fit body and clear mind. – **ANNA**

Being able to exercise is a blessing. It can be a real joy to live in a body that is strong and full of energy. However, not all of us take to exercise easily.

When we are out of shape, getting fit can seem like climbing a mountain. To get moving, follow these simple guidelines:

❈ Consider what form of exercise you enjoy. Start with small manageable steps and be consistent.
❈ Build activity into the rhythm of your day: stretching at home in the morning, walking or cycling to work, using stairs instead of lifts, parking the car a couple of blocks from the shops and walking the rest of the way.
❈ Regular moderate exercise is the key. Aim to gradually include physical activities that develop these four valuable components of fitness:
  ❧ Flexibility
  ❧ Muscle strength and tone
  ❧ Cardiovascular fitness
  ❧ Core strength.

Fitness is about developing balance in the body. Things to avoid include:

❈ Focusing exclusively on one type of exercise. For example, running or cycling can create muscle imbalances in the body, leading to a possible injury.
❈ Over-exercising. Constant pain, deep exhaustion or a decline in physical health are all signs that the body needs rest.
❈ Overworking your body. It will stress your adrenal system and may make you susceptible to illness, injury and premature ageing.

We enjoy the combination of yoga (for strengthening, toning muscles, and flexibility) and hill walking or cycling (for cardiovascular fitness and stamina).

2. BREATHE DEEPLY

Breathing deeply is the quickest way to improve how you feel. Taking slow, full and rhythmic breaths triggers the 'relaxation response' in the parasympathetic nervous system, reducing the heart rate and calming the mind. Increased levels of oxygen can also help alleviate anxiety and depression.

Yoga and yogic breathing exercises, T'ai Chi, qi gong, singing and meditation are ideal ways to improve breathing. A wonderful side-effect of improved breathing is a feeling of greater peace and calm.

If you work in an office, use Post-it notes or a computer timer to remind you to breathe deeply. Just three full breaths can reduce stress and promote a more relaxed feeling. Make time for a walk outdoors at lunchtime and take regular micro-breaks to stretch your arms and shoulders.

3. DETOXIFY NATURALLY

We are all exposed to toxins in food, air and water while other toxins are created within the body. Thankfully, the human body has a range of mechanisms for recognising and eliminating unhelpful toxins. Eating well and reducing stress definitely helps the detoxification process.

Here are some simple ways to improve your body's natural detoxification ability:

※ Eat a wholefood diet that includes plenty of fresh vegetables, fruit and protein.
※ Eat raw green leafy vegetables regularly.
※ Drink plenty of pure water every day.
※ Begin each day with a moist, easily digested breakfast, followed by a substantial, balanced lunch and finish with a light dinner to give your digestive system a good rest at night.
※ When you experience a loss of appetite, listen to your body. Sometimes your body needs a break from digesting food to cleanse and heal itself. However, in the case of persistent loss of appetite or rapid weight loss, always seek advice from a doctor.
※ If you are planning to undertake a detox programme, seek appropriate advice and supervision before beginning.

4. FEEL THE SUNSHINE

Although overexposure to radiation from the sun can damage skin and lead to premature ageing and skin cancer, careful, limited exposure to sunshine brings many positive benefits. Sunlight stimulates the production of serotonin (the feel-good hormone) and melatonin (the sleep-well hormone). Some skin conditions, including acne and psoriasis, can improve with moderate sun exposure. Here are some tips for enjoying safe exposure to sunlight:

※ In summer, avoid direct sun between 10am and 3pm.
※ Wear a hat and apply sunscreen to exposed areas of your body when outdoors.
※ Exercise caution and avoid burning at all times.
※ Eat plenty of fresh antioxidant-rich wholefoods to nourish and protect skin cells.

5. FEED YOUR SKIN

A varied diet of high-quality natural foods is truly the best skincare regime available – working from the inside out – but when you do choose skincare products and cosmetics always look for natural products. Certain chemicals in conventional products are proven carcinogens (cancer-causing). Others are endocrine disruptors, meaning they interfere with hormone production and function, and with foetal development. Buy antiperspirants, cosmetics, perfumes, skincare products and shampoos that are organic or at least made with natural non-synthetic ingredients.

6. CREATE A HEALTHY HOME

Effective preventative healthcare includes using natural building materials, paints, furnishings and cleaning products. Here are some other things you can do:

❅ Replace chemical cleaners, laundry powder, dishwashing powder, air fresheners, paints and pesticides with eco-friendly products, or learn about simple, old-fashioned alternatives. Baking soda, lemon juice, vinegar, and plain soap are sufficient for most household cleaning jobs.
❅ Avoid storing or heating food, especially fatty products, in soft plastic containers or cling film.
❅ Exchange stale air for fresh air a couple of times a day. Cross-ventilate by leaving windows open on both sides of the house.
❅ If building or renovating a home, use eco-friendly building materials, paints, furnishings and floor coverings. Consider installing a water-filter system for the whole house to eliminate chlorine and other chemicals.
❅ Always check for toxins, such as lead-based paints and asbestos, in any old building being renovated.

7. GO EARLY TO BED

One of our friends sets her alarm for the evening – to help her get to bed early!
Getting plenty of sleep supports good health on many levels.

Lack of sleep contributes to stress-related illnesses, erodes general health and reduces the speed of recovery from illness and injury. Here are our tips for getting plenty of sleep:

❅ Go to bed at the first yawn. Your body is programmed to physically repair and regenerate most efficiently between 10pm and 2am.
❅ Choose relaxing low-tech evening activities. Avoid flickering screens in the last hour or so before bed. Use softer lights after dark.
❅ Eat a light dinner several hours before going to bed.
❅ Minimise sweet treats in the evening.
❅ Exercise regularly to relieve stress and clear the mind.
❅ Try a few gentle stretches and/or slow deep-breathing exercises before bed.

8. DEVELOP LOVE AND RESPECT

Having good friends is not only one of life's greatest joys, but researchers have shown it also improves general health and life expectancy. However, it is only possible to create caring and rewarding relationships when you know, on a deep level, that you are worthy and lovable. When you respect yourself, you naturally gain respect and interest from others.

In a nourishing relationship there is safety, mutual respect and a sense of trust; we are able to speak freely even when there are disagreements; there is joy, humour and room to evolve and grow. However, these relationships don't just happen by themselves. You need to actively create them. Good communication is the most important ingredient in a healthy relationship and can bring fresh energy to even the most difficult ones. Find out about NVC (non-violent communication), a global network committed to improving communication and resolving conflict.

9. CULTIVATE CALM

An optimistic and relaxed mind promotes good health and well-being, while chronic negative thinking and unresolved past experiences can contribute to serious illness. It takes patience and sometimes outside help to understand all our thoughts and shifting emotions; however, it can be a deeply rewarding process.

Try this simple meditation technique for just 10 minutes:
* Get comfortable in an attentive, upright posture and close your eyes.
* Become aware of the contact of your body with the chair or floor.
* Turn your attention to your breathing.
* When you notice your attention has wandered, gently return to your breathing.

Meditating daily helps relieve stress and tension, develops calm and mental clarity and inevitably improves your health and well-being. Try it while walking, gardening or doing the household chores. To learn more about meditation, see our website: www.wildhealthfood.com/learn-to-meditate

10. ENJOY LIFE

Treat yourself with regular indulgences in the things that make you feel relaxed and truly happy. Whether it's walking in nature, surfing, going fishing or working in your garden, it's important to make space for the things you love. Consider ways of bringing nourishing activities into everyday life.

Don't ask yourself what the world needs, ask yourself what makes you come alive, then go and do that. Because what the world needs is people who have come alive. – **HAROLD WHITMAN**

What is a healthy diet?

A healthy diet does not mean following a strict eating plan for a couple of weeks in order to lose weight. It is about having a healthy relationship with food that sustains, nourishes and sets you up for a happy and balanced life. As we are all different, so our individual eating patterns will also be unique. The diet that works for your spouse, your best friend or Dr Robert Atkins may not suit you. Experiment and learn which foods help you feel your best.

You're probably thinking that you need to be a nutritional scientist and calculate the right percentages of fat and carbohydrates to create a healthy balanced meal. It's actually much easier and a lot more fun than that. You may be surprised to learn that you don't always have to eat healthy food to enjoy full health. Making fresh, wholesome food for at least 80% of your diet will provide your body with a firm nutritional foundation.

A BALANCED MEAL

A healthy meal includes something from each of the following four food groups:

Non-starchy vegetables

Making non-starchy vegetables a large part of your diet is essential for optimum health. These include leafy greens, courgettes, capsicums (peppers), celery and broccoli. See page 57 for a more comprehensive list.

Starchy vegetables, grains or beans

Complex carbohydrates are the starches found in wholefoods such as grains, beans, fruit and vegetables, such as kumara (sweet potato), pumpkin and potato. They provide longer-lasting energy than refined grains and sugars. Eating simple sugars and white starches, such as white rice and flour-based products (breads, pasta, pastries, etc.), causes abnormal blood-sugar fluctuations. In the longer term, this can lead to insulin resistance, obesity, type-2 diabetes and heart disease.

Healthy fats and oils

Healthy fats provide energy but are also vital for insulation, healthy skin, and nerve and brain function. The best sources of healthy fats are oily fish such as salmon, tuna and sardines. It is a good idea to eat oily fish two or three times a week. It is also a good idea to eat seeds and nuts most days.

Try cold-pressed hemp or flaxseed oil in dressings for a change. You may prefer to take fish and seed oil supplements, but visit a health-food store for advice first. Cold-pressed olive oil, organic butter, sesame and extra virgin coconut oil are other good sources of healthy fats.

Protein

Protein provides amino acids, the building blocks required for tissue growth and repair. However, protein is also essential for detoxification, hormone production, immune function and the nervous system. Include rich sources of protein in every meal, such as fish, meat, nuts, seeds, eggs, dairy products, grains and beans.

FOODS TO AVOID

We recommend that you avoid cheap, bulk vegetable oils and all deep-fried foods. Polyunsaturated oils, such as sunflower, corn, safflower and canola, are easily damaged by light and heat; buy only cold-pressed oils and store in the dark. Fizzy drinks, products baked with white flour, refined sugars, processed diet foods, processed meats, and foods containing MSG and food colouring should also be avoided.

SHOPPING GUIDE

Making good food a priority in your budget is a form of health insurance for you and your family. Here are some key points to consider:

* Buy locally grown fresh vegetables and fruit or, even better, grow your own.
* Choose certified organic foods. Not only are they free of chemical toxins, they generally have a higher nutritional quality.
* Look for a farmers' market in your area where you will be able to talk to the people who grow, farm and process the food on sale.
* At the supermarket, select most of your food from the peripheries of the store. Generally, processed foods dominate the central aisles and the fresh foods line the walls.
* Read food labels carefully. Choose packaged foods made with natural, recognisable ingredients and the fewest additives. Avoid products containing refined sugar.
* Nuts, seeds, grains, beans and dried fruit can be expensive when purchased in small amounts at supermarkets. For better quality, freshness and lower prices order direct from organic and natural food suppliers.

There is a lot more we could say about the subject of nutrition but such discussion is beyond the scope of this book. For more information, please go to our website: www.wildhealthfood.com

USING OUR RECIPES

The recipes in this book are based on fresh, wholefood ingredients, full of flavour and easy to prepare. They are offered as inspiration and motivation to explore your food choices rather than as a rigid prescription for what or how you should eat. We have included some unusual ingredients at times to bring greater variety into everyday meals. However, we guarantee that all are tried and true as we are sharing some of our favourite home-cooking ideas with you.

We have put a lot of effort into making our recipes simple, clear and accurate. Some cooks may not wish to measure everything and most recipes will come out fine with a little variation. Having said that, we recommend you measure ingredients carefully when making baked desserts and when adding seasonings, in particular salt and spices.

A blender or food processor is required for some of our recipes. These machines can save you a lot of time in the kitchen, enabling healthy food to be prepared much faster. We recommend investing in strong, long-lasting equipment.

The ❋ symbol marks steps to be done well ahead of time, such as soaking nuts overnight.

If you don't feel confident in the kitchen, take heart. Cooking is a basic skill that anyone can learn. Curiosity, careful attention, playfulness and patience are qualities that will help you learn to make great-tasting food.

SEASONING

Processed packaged foods generally have extreme flavours – usually salty or sweet – and are designed to stimulate cravings for more. Food made from natural ingredients, on the other hand, that have been carefully seasoned are nourishing and satisfying. Most well-loved traditional dishes are popular because they have a good balance of flavours.

When a dish tastes flat, it is likely to need a little sea salt. Add salt a pinch at a time and taste after each addition to ensure the flavours are just right.

Try any of the following natural seasonings in your cooking:

- ❀ Honey, sugar and dried fruit for added sweetness.
- ❀ Salt, miso and shoyu (soy sauce) for saltiness and to draw out existing flavours in the dish.
- ❀ Lemon zest and juice, vinegar and tamarind paste for a touch of piquancy.
- ❀ Black pepper, garlic, chilli and ginger for added spice.

NUTS AND SEEDS

Nuts and seeds are a wonderful source of protein, healthy fats and minerals. In their raw form, however, they are difficult to digest. Many of our recipes use nuts, seeds or grains that have been soaked in water for several hours or overnight. Rehydrating the nuts and seeds makes them more nutritious.

How to soak nuts:

- ❀ Place in a bowl, then cover with plenty of water.
- ❀ Leave larger nuts, such as almonds, hazelnuts and cashews, to soak overnight. Smaller seeds, such as sunflower seeds, may be ready to use after 3 or 4 hours.
- ❀ Drain and rinse the nuts or seeds before use.
- ❀ Surplus soaked and drained nuts will keep for several days in the refrigerator. They can be used in salads, as snacks or added to a lunchbox. Even small shoots can be used in salads. Soaked nuts and seeds can also be frozen and thawed in warm water, as required.

Something I've always loved about Anna is the way she can turn the simplest meal into a special occasion. She may put flowers on the table, light a candle, or pause to say some words of gratitude before eating. Nowadays, these little rituals help keep us sane amidst the chaos of feeding a hungry baby boy. – **ROGER**

Eating in a relaxed atmosphere can aid digestion. By taking time to appreciate the colours, flavour and texture of the food you are eating, you are also more likely to know when you have eaten enough.

TIME TO EAT

So, now we have passed on a few of our ideas for introducing your body to a healthier diet, it's time to get creative in the kitchen!

Breakfasts

One of our best friends, Rachel, used to skip breakfast most days. By mid-morning she would start to feel shaky due to low blood-sugar levels. She felt that she couldn't think clearly and her brain would 'stop working'. Sugar cravings would then lead her to binge on something sweet. This would cause what Rachel called a 'fizz-bomb' – an initial sugar hit and energy rush, followed by a crash, leading to emotional instability. Eventually she wised up. These days Rachel eats a good balanced breakfast and finds she has stable energy right through to lunch. Eggs scrambled with vegetables are a regular favourite. – ANNA

You may have heard the German proverb, 'Eat breakfast like a king, lunch like a prince and dinner like a pauper'. It's true, breakfast is indeed the most important meal of the day.

A good breakfast will activate your metabolism, refuel hungry cells and get you through the morning energised and clear-headed. Skipping breakfast and ending the day with a huge dinner, on the other hand, is more likely to result in weight gain.

A good-quality breakfast can be quick to make once you get into the habit of soaking grains the evening before. Alternatively, a nutritious, filling smoothie can be made in a few minutes and enjoyed while travelling or at work.

OUR RECOMMENDATIONS FOR A NOURISHING BREAKFAST:

* Eat food that makes you feel energised and satisfied.
* Moist food such as Bircher muesli, a fruit smoothie or soft-cooked eggs are ideal for easy digestion.
* Ensure the meal contains sufficient protein and healthy fats to prevent overeating later in the day.
* Whole grains such as oats, quinoa, buckwheat and millet may be cooked fresh or reheated from the night before. Add yoghurt or eggs for extra protein.

Avoid store-bought breakfast cereals and refined breads. While shaking cereal out of a packet and pouring milk over the top is certainly quick, it is not the healthiest choice for breakfast. Most boxed cereals are high in refined sugar and lack substance. Many are hard, dry and difficult to digest.

BREAKFAST SUPERFOODS

Include some of the following in your breakfast and you should make it through the whole day with a feeling of well-being:

* Bee pollen – sprinkle on porridge or muesli, or add to smoothies.
* Freshly ground pumpkin seeds, sunflower seeds and flaxseeds – sprinkle on porridge or grains.
* Green powders, such as spirulina, chorella or barley grass – add to water, juice or fruit smoothies. Ensure you choose high-quality brands.
* Molasses is an excellent replacement for other refined sugars and a good source of minerals, including iron – pour a little on porridge or grains for extra sweetness.
* Homemade coriander or basil pesto – spread on toast or spoon on top of eggs.
* Unhulled tahini is a good source of calcium and good-quality oils – spread on wholegrain toast or add to smoothies.

Bircher muesli

Eaten all year round in our house, this simple soaked muesli is one of our favourite breakfasts. It is deliciously creamy, especially if made with organic rolled oats, and contains a rich variety of foods, providing broad nutrition to get us through the day ahead.

8 cups (800g) organic rolled oats
1 cup sunflower seeds
⅓ cup pumpkin seeds
½ cup dried coconut
1 cup (180g) mixed dried fruit, chopped
    or sliced as required
1 tablespoon ground cinnamon

OPTIONAL EXTRAS
½ cup cashew nut pieces
1 cup whole buckwheat
1 tablespoon five-spice powder

FOR SERVING
lemon juice
fresh fruit
Greek yoghurt
ground flaxseed
bee pollen (optional)

☀ Mix dry ingredients together in a big bowl. Store in a large jar or other airtight container. Each evening, place about ⅔ cup per serving required in a bowl. Add about ½ cup water per serving – just enough to cover the muesli. Leave to soak overnight.

In the morning, mix in a little lemon juice and chopped or grated fresh fruit. Serve in individual bowls. Top with yoghurt, ground flaxseed and bee pollen, if desired.

MAKES 20 SERVINGS

Brown rice and pomegranate muesli

The cheerful explosion of blood-red pomegranate seeds and the enlivening lift of orange and lemon zest make this a very merry breakfast indeed! For the seeds and nuts, try a mix of pumpkin seeds, almonds and cashews.

⅓ cup seeds and nuts
16 dried apricots or 8 ripe fresh apricots
2 pomegranates
2 cups cooked brown rice
rind of ½ small orange, finely diced
rind of ½ small lemon, finely diced

FOR SERVING
Greek yoghurt

☀ Soak nuts and seeds overnight in plenty of water. If using dried apricots, soak them overnight with just enough water to cover.

Drain apricots, but retain soaking juice. Slice apricots. Drain and rinse nuts and seeds.

Remove seeds from the pomegranate, discarding all the bitter white pith.

Mix all ingredients in a bowl, with half the apricot soaking juice.

Serve in individual bowls. Top with a dollop of Greek yoghurt. Alternatively, make a thick version of *Raspberry avocado smoothie* (see page 132), omitting the water to make a dense cream.

SERVES 4

TIME-SAVING TIPS FOR BREAKFAST
☀ When cooking grains for dinner, cook extra for breakfast, too.
☀ Remember to soak Bircher muesli, porridge oats or other grains overnight. Whole oats take just 5 minutes to cook when soaked and taste much creamier.
☀ No time to sit down and eat? Take a smoothie in a sipper cup to have at work.

Banana berry muffins

These wheat-free muffins have banana, sultanas and a pinch of stevia powder for sweetening. They are suitable for people who like to bake now and again, but wish to reduce their sugar intake.

2 cups spelt flour
1½ teaspoons baking powder
½ teaspoon baking soda
¼ teaspoon stevia powder
1 cup oat bran
60g melted butter or ¼ cup rice bran oil
½ cup natural yoghurt
2 eggs
1 cup milk (or rice milk or soy milk)
1 large ripe banana, mashed
1½ cups frozen raspberries or blueberries
½ cup sultanas

Heat oven to 180°C. Grease muffin tray.

Sift flour, baking powder, baking soda and stevia into a bowl. Mix in oat bran.

In a separate bowl, mix wet ingredients. Add to dry ingredients and mix together until just combined. Add the fruit and gently fold in.

Three-quarters-fill the muffin tins. Bake for approximately 15 minutes until golden and firm.

MAKES 12 MUFFINS

Whole oat porridge

During winter, porridge is a warm and satisfying breakfast. Plain porridge can be made more interesting with the addition of dried fruit, nuts or seeds. Here are a couple of our favourite variations.

OPTION 1: FIVE-SPICE PORRIDGE
1 cup wholegrain rolled oats
2 tablespoons sunflower seeds
3 tablespoons dried currants or raisins
½ teaspoon five-spice powder
small pinch of sea salt
2½ cups water

OPTION 2: APRICOT AND ALMOND PORRIDGE
1 cup wholegrain rolled oats
2 tablespoons raw almonds, whole
  or chopped
¼ cup dried apricots (about 8 whole),
  sliced or chopped
½ teaspoon ground cinnamon
small pinch of sea salt
2½ cups water

☀ Combine all ingredients in a saucepan and leave to soak overnight.

In the morning, place saucepan over a medium heat. Bring slowly to a boil, then cook for several minutes until thick and creamy.

Serve with favourite breakfast toppings, such as yoghurt, milk, fresh fruit, honey, or ground flaxseed.

BOTH RECIPES SERVE 2

Many studies have proven the benefits of eating high-fibre whole grains, such as oats, including reducing the risk of heart attack, cancer, stroke, obesity, and premature death. The fibre in oats is known to enhance immune function and help balance blood sugars. Oats are also helpful for calming the nervous system.

Banana berry muffins

Fresh fruit quinoa muesli

Quinoa is protein-rich, gluten-free and easily digested. The quinoa, nuts and seeds in this muesli combined with fruit create a balanced, sustaining breakfast.

⅓ cup sunflower seeds
⅓ cup cashew nut pieces
⅓ cup dried apricots, sliced
 3 cups cooked quinoa (made from 1 cup
   dry quinoa)
1 banana, chopped
1 large orange, peeled and chopped
½ teaspoon ground cinnamon
¼ teaspoon ginger powder
pinch of sea salt

☀ Place the sunflower seeds and cashew pieces in a small bowl. Cover with plenty of water. In another bowl, place the sliced apricots and add just enough water to cover. Leave to soak overnight.

In the morning, drain and rinse sunflower seeds and cashews.

Using a large spoon, mix together all ingredients until combined.

Serve muesli on its own or with yoghurt.

SERVES 6

Migas

There are many variations of this popular Spanish/Tex-Mex dish and the common ingredient is crumbled leftover bread or tortilla (migas).

4 eggs
¼ cup water
pinch of sea salt
dash of hot chilli sauce
2 wheat-free corn tortillas
2 tablespoons rice bran oil or clarified butter
2 chorizo sausages, sliced
¼ large red onion, diced
¼ red or green capsicum, deseeded and diced

Whisk egg, water, salt and chilli sauce together.

Tear tortillas into small pieces, roughly 2–3cm wide.

Heat oil or butter in a large frying pan. Fry chorizo until slightly browned. Remove to a small bowl. Add tortilla pieces to pan and fry until crispy. Remove tortilla and fry vegetables until soft. Add a little water to steam vegetables if they stick.

Pour egg mixture into frying pan with the vegetables. Add tortilla and chorizo pieces. Continue to cook over medium-low heat, stirring occasionally, until eggs are cooked but still moist.

Serve as is, or with any of the following additions: tomato slices, diced avocado, chopped jalapeño peppers, tomato salsa, chopped coriander and/or refried beans.

SERVES 2

Eggs are a wonderful source of affordable high-quality protein and they help balance blood sugar. Eating a breakfast that includes protein rather than just cereal can assist in weight loss because the appetite is satisfied for longer. If possible, buy eggs from free-range chickens – chickens that forage on green leaves and insects lay eggs that are more nutritious and contain higher levels of omega oils.

Migas

Buckwheat pancakes with blueberry apple compote

At our house these low-gluten pancakes are a fun weekend treat. Often we top them with fresh fruit and yoghurt; however, this blueberry compote also makes a warming winter breakfast. We soak the flours overnight to improve the texture of the pancakes and make the grains easier to digest.

BUCKWHEAT PANCAKES
½ cup buckwheat flour
½ cup wholemeal spelt flour
1 cup water
juice of 1 lemon
1 egg
¼ teaspoon sea salt
½ teaspoon baking soda
1 tablespoon melted butter or olive oil
butter or oil, for frying

COMPOTE
2 large eating apples, peeled and cut into
 1.5cm cubes
1 teaspoon honey
pinch of sea salt
½ cup water
1 cup frozen blueberries
2 teaspoons arrowroot powder

☀ Mix flours, water and lemon juice together in a bowl. Cover with a plate and leave overnight (6-12 hours). When ready to cook, add egg, salt, baking soda and butter or oil. Whisk to form a smooth batter.

To make the compote, put apple, honey, sea salt and ¼ cup water in a saucepan and bring to a boil. Cover with a lid and turn down heat. Simmer until apples are just starting to soften. Add blueberries and cook for a few more minutes until berries are warm.

Combine remaining water with arrowroot powder to form a smooth paste and stir into the hot mixture. Simmer for 1-2 minutes until mixture thickens. Remove from heat.

Heat a frying pan over medium heat and add 1 teaspoon butter or olive oil. Drop in a big spoonful of batter, then tip the pan, spreading mixture to form a large circle. Allow each pancake to cook until bubbles appear across the whole surface before turning over to complete cooking. Adjust heat as you go to ensure the pancakes have time to cook through without getting too dark. Stack cooked pancakes on a plate in a warming drawer or low oven until required.

Reheat compote if necessary. Serve pancakes with compote on individual plates topped with yoghurt.

MAKES 6 PANCAKES

Superfood breakfast smoothie

For a well-balanced breakfast that is easy to prepare, use this simple guide to create your own unique super breakfast smoothie.

1–1½ cups chopped fruit (apple, pear, orange,
 banana, peach, mango or berries)
1–2 parts protein (¼ cup natural yoghurt, handful
 of pumpkin seeds, sunflower seeds or almonds
 soaked overnight and drained, 1 organic free-
 range egg, 2 tablespoons whey protein powder)
1 part fat or oil (1 tablespoon flaxseed oil, ground
 flaxseed or sesame seeds, 2–3 teaspoons tahini,
 or 1 medium-sized avocado)
1 part superfood (1–2 teaspoons spirulina or multi-
 green powder, or 1 teaspoon bee pollen)

Place all ingredients in a blender and blend on high speed. Add water or milk to form a thick but drinkable smoothie.

Serve immediately or pour into a large travel cup for breakfast on-the-go.

SERVES 1

Buckwheat pancakes with blueberry apple compote

Lunches & snacks

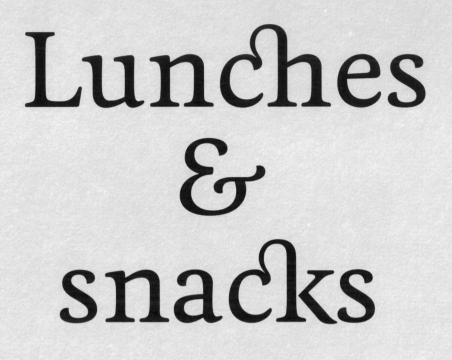

In my early twenties, while living in a Japanese Zen temple, I would join the monks on their weekly alms round. We walked all day in straw sandals, collecting offerings. At midday, as we rested our tired legs, our simple lunch of brown rice balls, nori and pickles tasted so delicious. – **ROGER**

The ideal lunch is a balanced combination of wholefoods, including fresh vegetables and some form of protein to maintain energy levels for the rest of the day. While it is quite possible that a wholesome sandwich fits the bill, the recipes in this chapter should provide some delicious alternatives.

For most of us the big question is how to eat well when away from home: at work, school, out shopping or on the road.

HOMEMADE LUNCHES

The most reliable way to eat a good lunch is to make it at home and take it with you. Homemade food costs less and you'll know exactly what you're eating. Weekend preparation of soups in winter and dips and spreads in summer makes weekday lunches a breeze.

Our easiest home-takeaway lunch is a combination of salad leaves with add-ons. We like hummus, leftover cold meat, canned wild salmon, hard-boiled eggs, nuts and seeds, grated vegetables, avocado, cooked grains, cooked or sprouted beans, and fresh herbs. If you like, take the dressing in a small container to drizzle over before eating.

We also enjoy sandwiches. Slow-fermented sourdough is the easiest bread to digest and maximises mineral absorption. Low-wheat flatbreads for wraps are another good option. Alternatively, wraps can be made using sheets of nori seaweed. For fillings use dips or spreads, plenty of fresh salad vegetables and some good-quality protein. Here are some of our favourite combinations:

* Free-range ham with mustard, cheese, lettuce and tomato
* Boiled egg, mashed with fresh herbs or curry, and a little sour cream
* Sprouts, hummus and homemade chutney
* Sardines, tomato and rocket
* Cold free-range chicken with sun-dried tomato spread and lettuce
* Tahini or almond butter with sliced bananas and cinnamon
* Guacamole with lettuce, tomato and cheese
* Coriander or wild weed pesto with smoked fish and green leaves.

BOUGHT LUNCHES

Most often the cheapest lunch options are loaded with carbohydrates and lack real nutrition. At the average café or bakery we find pies, pastries, pizzas, pasta, burgers, bagels, buns, sandwiches, rolls, wraps, muffins, cakes and biscuits. Dry long-life snack foods generally contain unhealthy fats and a long list of chemical additives. Deep-fried foods, although warm and tempting, provide only short-term energy and are full of toxic, overheated oils.

If there is no choice but to buy lunch, be prepared to pay a little more for freshness and quality. Here are some suggestions:

* Fresh soup
* Hearty salads with lots of fresh vegetables and quality protein, such as fish and eggs
* Smoothies that include fruit, protein and healthy fats, such as yoghurt
* Fresh juice (as part of a meal)
* Wholegrain sandwiches with plenty of salad inside.

Wild weed pesto

Most wild greens have a strong, bitter flavour but you'll be amazed how combining them with olive oil and seeds can make a delicious pesto. The recipe works well with many other greens, such as rocket, coriander and spinach, and can also be spiced up with fresh chilli.

1 cup pumpkin seeds, soaked overnight ☀
2 cups (packed) chickweed, puha or other mild-
 tasting edible weeds
3 cloves garlic, chopped
¼ cup olive oil
2 tablespoons miso (or ½ teaspoon sea salt)
2 tablespoons lemon juice

Drain and rinse pumpkin seeds.

Wash weeds or greens, drain well, then chop roughly.

Place in a food processor with soaked pumpkin seeds and remaining ingredients. Process until well combined.

MAKES 2 CUPS

Roast pumpkin hummus

600g pumpkin, peeled, deseeded and cut into
 large chunks
2 cups cooked chickpeas
2 tablespoons tahini
1 teaspoon ground cumin
1 teaspoon ground coriander
1–2 teaspoons chilli sauce
juice of 1 lemon
4 cloves garlic, chopped
1 teaspoon sea salt

Place pumpkin in a lightly oiled oven dish. Cover with foil. Bake in a moderate (180°C) oven until completely soft. A few darkened edges are fine.

When pumpkin is cool, place in a food processor with remaining ingredients. Blend until smooth. If necessary, add water to adjust consistency.

MAKES 3½ CUPS

Feeling sleepy in the afternoon? Go easy on grain- and carbohydrate-heavy meals in the middle of the day. Even sushi can be too heavy for some people. Instead, try salad- or vegetable-based lunches that include some protein. Reducing portion size or eating several smaller snacks instead of a large lunch may also help.

Coriander pesto

Pomegranate molasses and chilli sauce give this pesto real character. Spread on toast, dollop onto steamed vegetables, serve with fish or use to garnish a soup.

1 cup coriander (packed), roots trimmed, washed and coarsely chopped
½ cup cashew nut pieces
½ cup dried coconut
3 cloves garlic, chopped
¼ cup olive oil
2 teaspoons pomegranate molasses (or lemon juice)
½–1 teaspoon chilli sauce
½ teaspoon sea salt

Place coriander, cashew pieces, coconut and garlic in a food processor. Blend on high until everything is finely chopped.

Add olive oil, pomegranate molasses, chilli sauce and sea salt. Continue to blend until well combined.

Leftovers will keep for up to 10 days in a glass jar with an airtight lid. Alternatively, freeze in ready-to-use portions; ice-cube trays are ideal for this.

MAKES 1½ CUPS

Coriander is a powerful detoxifier which can help cleanse body tissues and remove heavy metals from the body. Coriander has also been shown to act as an anti-inflammatory and to help control blood-sugar levels.

Curried carrot dip

⅔ cup cashew nuts, soaked overnight ☀
1½ cups grated carrot
¼ cup coconut cream
1 teaspoon Thai red curry paste
1 tablespoon tamarind paste (or 2 teaspoons lemon juice)
⅓ teaspoon sea salt

Drain and rinse cashew nuts.

Place all ingredients in a food processor or blender. Blend until well combined.

MAKES 2 CUPS

Coconut spinach dip

½ cup sunflower seeds, soaked overnight ☀
2 cups (packed) spinach leaves
⅓ cup dried coconut
¼ cup coconut cream
1 orange, peeled and chopped
5 dates, pitted and chopped
small pinch of cayenne pepper
⅓ teaspoon sea salt

Drain and rinse sunflower seeds.

Place seeds in a food processor with remaining ingredients. Blend until smooth.

MAKES 2½ CUPS

Fave feta fiesta

Broad beans have a bad reputation in many homes, thanks to the tough, grey, overcooked beans our mothers dished up. The Italians, who call them 'fave', usually eat them young, fresh and peeled. This bright and tasty dip will erase bad memories!

250g frozen broad beans
250g frozen green peas
1 fresh chilli, deseeded and chopped (or a dash of chilli sauce)
2 tablespoons extra virgin olive oil
1 tablespoon lemon juice
½ teaspoon sea salt
100g feta cheese, crumbled or cubed
large handful mint, roughly chopped

In separate bowls, allow broad beans and peas to thaw. (If in a hurry, cover broad beans and peas with boiling water, leave for 2 minutes, then drain.)

Remove broad bean skins by splitting one end with a fingernail, then squeezing out the green kernels inside. Discard skins.

Place peas, chilli, olive oil, lemon juice and salt in a food processor. Process until well combined. Add broad beans and pulse briefly, leaving as much texture as you prefer.

Tip mixture into a bowl. Mix in feta and chopped mint.

MAKES 2½ CUPS

Tofu and mushroom rissoles

This is a handy way to use leftover rice. Easy finger-food and fine eaten cold, the mushroom balls look stunning decorated with black and white sesame seeds, but will taste as good with just one colour.

⅔ cup flaxseed
1 red onion, roughly chopped
1 tablespoon fresh thyme, chopped
300g mushrooms, roughly chopped
300g firm tofu
3 cups cooked rice (from 1 cup dry rice)
1 teaspoon sea salt
3 tablespoons shoyu
¼ cup white sesame seeds
¼ cup black sesame seeds

Grind flaxseed in a spice grinder until fine. You may need to do this in several batches.

Place red onion and thyme in a food processor (with S blade) and pulse until fine. Add mushroom and pulse-chop again for a few seconds until fine but not completely minced. Transfer mixture into a bowl.

Break up tofu and add to the bowl. Mash tofu by squeezing through fingers. Add cooked rice, ground flaxseed, salt and shoyu. Mix well. Form mixture into balls, a bit larger than golf-ball size, using your hands to press firmly into shape. Place balls on a tray.

Put black and white sesame seeds into two separate bowls. Dip one side of each ball into the white seeds, then turn over and dip into black. Place mushroom-tofu balls on an oven tray.

Bake at 180°C for 25 minutes or until firm.

Serve with a rich tomato-based pasta sauce.

(For a variation, add 6–8 chopped sun-dried tomatoes or ⅓ cup of pitted and sliced black olives.)

SERVES 6 AS A LUNCH WITH SALAD

Baba ghannouj

In the Middle East, this purée is traditionally made by roasting small eggplants over an open flame until charred on the outside and soft inside. Try this over a gas ring or barbecue grill.

1kg eggplants
juice of 2 medium lemons (3 tablespoons)
4 tablespoons tahini
2-4 cloves garlic
1 teaspoon sea salt
small handful of parsley, roughly chopped

Heat oven to 200°C. Pierce skins of the eggplants in several places with a fork. Place on a baking tray. Bake for 30-40 minutes until soft inside. Remove and allow to cool.

When eggplants are cool enough to handle, scoop out the flesh. Put flesh into a food processor. Add lemon juice, tahini, garlic and sea salt. Blend until smooth.

Add parsley and process for a few moments more.

Serve either as a dip, drizzled with a little olive oil, or a sandwich spread. Alternatively, add stock or water - enough to turn into a soup and heat to serve.

MAKES 3 CUPS

Beetroot tamarind dip

⅔ cup sunflower seeds, soaked overnight ☀
2-3 small beetroots (200g)
3 tablespoons tamarind paste or 2 tablespoons lemon juice
1 knob ginger, sliced
1 apple, chopped
1 tablespoon miso
1 teaspoon chilli sauce (optional)

Drain and rinse sunflower seeds.

Grate beetroot using a hand grater or food processor.

Combine all ingredients in a food processor. Blend as smooth as possible.

MAKES 2½ CUPS

Cashew cheese

Here's a wonderful non-dairy substitute for cream cheese or ricotta. It takes at least 24 hours to ferment, but the process is very simple.

1½ cups cashews (whole or pieces),
  soaked overnight ☀
juice of 1 lemon
¼ cup water
½ teaspoon sea salt

Drain and rinse cashews.

Combine all ingredients in a food processor. Blend until fairly smooth. Add a little more water, if necessary, to get the mixture to combine.

Line a sieve with cheesecloth. Place over a bowl. Transfer cashew mixture into cheesecloth and fold surplus cloth over to cover. Leave in a warm place for 24–36 hours to ripen.

Remove cheese from cloth, transfer to a non-plastic container and cover. Refrigerate and use within 3 or 4 days.

MAKES 2 CUPS

The butter-versus-margarine debate continues, but we personally choose to eat good old-fashioned butter. Butter from grass-fed cows provides valuable fat-soluble vitamins A and D, and a good balance of omega-3 and omega-6.

Salmon salsa

A colourful five-minute lunch, packed with protein and omega-3 oils and featuring bright plump kernels of fresh corn which are delicious raw. If fresh corn is not available, use a small can of corn kernels.

1 cob fresh corn
185g can salmon, drained
½ red capsicum, diced
2 medium tomatoes, diced
1 medium avocado, diced
2 tablespoons olive oil
juice of 1 lemon (or 1 tablespoon
  cider vinegar)
dash of chilli sauce
½ teaspoon sea salt

Remove kernels of fresh corn by halving the cob, standing each piece on end, then slicing downwards.

Combine corn kernels in a bowl with remaining ingredients. Mix well.

SERVES 2

Farinata

Our version of farinata (traditionally a thin, crispy pancake) is more like a frittata, but made with chickpea flour instead of egg. Delicious hot or cold, it's perfect for a picnic or packed in lunchboxes for school or work.

CHICKPEA BATTER
250g chickpea flour
3 cups warm water
1 teaspoon ground cumin
1 teaspoon sea salt
juice of 1 lemon
75ml olive oil

FILLING
1 large eggplant (400g), cut in 2cm cubes
3 tablespoons olive oil
½ teaspoon sea salt
1 red onion, diced in large pieces
3 zucchini (300g), cut in 2cm chunks
3 tomatoes, roughly diced
chopped parsley or other fresh herbs
½ teaspoon chilli flakes (optional)

To make batter, sift chickpea flour into the water while whisking. Add cumin, sea salt and lemon juice. Leave in a warm place for about 2 hours. (The batter thickens slightly while resting.)

For the filling, heat oven to 180°C. In a large roasting dish, toss cubed eggplant with olive oil and salt. Roast for about 15 minutes until soft. Add red onion and zucchini and roast for about 10 minutes until zucchini has softened slightly. Remove from oven and add diced tomato and herbs.

Add olive oil to the chickpea batter. Whisk well, then pour evenly over the vegetables in roasting dish. Sprinkle with chilli flakes.

Return dish to oven and bake for 20–25 minutes until the centre feels firm to touch. Remove from oven and allow to cool for 10 minutes.

Cut into large squares and serve.

SERVES 6

Tamari roasted seeds

Eat these seeds on their own as a snack, or sprinkle onto salads or soups.

1 tablespoon tamari
pinch of cayenne pepper (optional)
¼ teaspoon garlic powder (optional)
1 cup sunflower or pumpkin seeds

Measure tamari into a small cup and add spices, if using.

Heat a heavy-based frying pan over moderate heat. Toast seeds, stirring constantly with a wooden spoon, until fragrant and slightly browned. Pumpkin seeds will swell and pop when ready.

Remove pan from heat and sprinkle tamari over hot seeds. Continue stirring. The remaining heat will cause tamari to dry onto seeds. Return briefly to the heat if necessary.

Allow seeds to cool, then store in an airtight jar for up to 2 weeks.

MAKES 1 CUP

The low-fat mantra of recent years is gradually being replaced by a low-carb message. Both sugars and starches from sweet foods and refined grains contribute to elevated glucose levels in the bloodstream. Consistently excessive blood sugar is recognised as a key contributor to the most serious health problems of the modern world: heart disease, obesity and diabetes.

Pan-roasted karengo with pumpkin seeds

This crunchy and satisfying snack is also delicious sprinkled on a simple green salad.

1 cup karengo
⅓ cup pumpkin or sunflower seeds
½ teaspoon olive oil

Warm a heavy-based frying pan over medium heat and add seeds. Toast for 5 minutes, stirring with a wooden spoon, until evenly browned and fragrant.

Lower heat. Add karengo and olive oil. Continue stirring for another 5 minutes or until karengo is shiny and crunchy.

Turn off heat and allow to cool in pan. Store in an airtight glass jar for up to 3 weeks.

MAKES 1⅓ CUPS

Edible seaweed contains a mega-dose of minerals necessary for optimum health. Get a daily dose of sea minerals by sprinkling karengo or shaking kelp powder on salads and veggies. Arame and hijiki are delicious in salads. Kombu can be added to cooking grains and beans to enrich with minerals and improve digestibility. Wakame is good in soups (notably miso). Most sea vegetables are easy to hide in soups and casseroles for fussy family members.

Rice balls

This is a popular lunchtime choice at Iku, the vegan macrobiotic takeaway in Sydney where Roger once worked. The rice balls at Iku are deep-fried but our version is baked with just a little oil.

70g sunflower seeds
40g sesame seeds
1 stalk celery
1 medium-sized carrot (150g), peeled or scrubbed
3 cups cooked brown rice (from 1 cup dry)
2 tablespoons shoyu
¼ cup wholemeal spelt flour
1 teaspoon sea salt
rice bran oil

Heat oven to 180°C.

Place seeds in a roasting dish and toast until lightly browned.

Finely chop the celery and carrot or pulse in a food processor using the S blade.

Put all ingredients in a big bowl and mix together with your hands. Squeeze into balls (a bit larger than golf-ball size). If the mixture is not sticky enough, try adding a little water and a bit more flour.

Dip one half of each ball into the oil and place each ball on a baking tray oil-side up (so the oil drips down over the ball).

Bake for 20 minutes at 180°C or until firm and golden.

Serve with a big salad and shoyu for dipping.

MAKES 9–10 BALLS (SERVES 4)

Gluten-free corn fritters

⅓ cup buckwheat flour
⅓ cup brown rice flour
½ teaspoon baking powder
2 eggs
¼ cup milk
pinch of sea salt
400g can corn kernels, drained
1 small onion, finely chopped and sautéed
   (optional)
chopped fresh parsley or coriander (optional)
100g feta cheese, cubed small (optional)
2 tablespoons rice bran oil (more or less)

Sift flours and baking powder into a large bowl.

Put egg, milk and salt in another bowl and whisk to combine. Stir in corn kernels and onion, and parsley and feta, if using.

Add wet mixture to the flours. Mix well.

Heat a heavy-based frying pan over a low-medium heat and add a little oil. Cook large spoonfuls of mixture for around 3 minutes on each side, or until golden brown and firm to touch.

Serve warm with sliced tomatoes, avocado and grilled bacon.

SERVES 4

A methodical elimination diet is the easiest way to test if a particular food is causing you problems. Try going without the suspected food for two weeks and note changes to your physical health, energy levels, mental clarity and emotional state. Reintroduce the food gradually and observe any changes in your well-being.

Karengo egg-fried rice

This is a quick way to use leftover rice and is popular with children and adults alike.

1 tablespoon karengo or wakame seaweed
1 tablespoon coconut oil or butter
2 red, yellow or orange capsicums, deseeded
   and diced
4 free-range eggs
200g frozen peas
4 spring onions, finely sliced
3 cups cooked rice (from 1 cup uncooked rice)
2 tablespoons tamari

Soak karengo in water for 10 minutes.

Heat oil or butter in a wok or large heavy-based frying pan. Add the capsicum and cook for a couple of minutes to let it start to soften.

Drain karengo.

Break eggs into the pan and stir-fry them so that they start to scramble, then stir in the peas, karengo and spring onion.

Add the cooked rice and continue heating and stirring until hot. Season with tamari and serve immediately.

SERVES 4

Silky spinach soup

A wonderful way to drink greens! Raw spinach tastes great in this soup full of live enzymes, antioxidants, healthy oils, minerals and vitamins. As with all raw soups, this one is tastiest served cold.

3 cups spinach leaves and stems (1 small bunch)
2 small zucchini (200g), chopped
1 medium apple, cored and chopped
1 avocado
1–2 cloves garlic, roughly chopped
2 tablespoons shoyu
½ teaspoon sea salt
1 tablespoon lemon juice
1 tablespoon olive oil
small pinch of cayenne pepper
1 cup water

Wash spinach leaves in plenty of water, then drain. Put in a food processor or strong blender with remaining ingredients. Blend until smooth.

Serve cold or hot, as desired.

SERVES 3–4

Raw soups have featured in the traditional cuisine of many cultures worldwide. Benefits include:
❀ Fresh and rich flavours
❀ An abundance of food enzymes that aid digestion
❀ Nutrients that are readily absorbed by the body
❀ Convenience as they are ready-to-consume treats.

Cucumber dill soup

We make this simple cold soup often over the summer months when there is an abundance of large, juicy cucumbers at our local farmers' market. Organically grown cucumbers have a complex, creamy, sweet flavour compared with their conventional cousins, and if they are available you can leave out the apple.

1 small bunch fresh dill
1 large telegraph cucumber, peeled and chopped
zest and juice of 1 small lemon
2 tablespoons olive oil
½ cup yoghurt
1 small apple, core removed and chopped
1–2 teaspoons sea salt
ground black pepper
extra olive oil for drizzling

Remove some of the fine dill tips, reserving these for garnish. Remove any tough stalks, then chop remaining dill.

Put all ingredients in a blender or food processor. Blend until smooth. If using a blender, a little water may be needed to help begin the process.

Adjust seasoning to taste.

Serve in individual bowls, garnished with a drizzle of olive oil and dill tips.

SERVES 4

Chicken, barley and lemon soup

Pearl barley, when cooked slowly, swells and thickens to give a lovely creamy texture to soups and stews. This soup is a nourishing and strengthening meal, ideal for anyone with a cold or recovering from illness.

1 tablespoon olive oil
1 large onion, chopped
500g diced fresh free-range chicken (thigh
   meat is best)
1 large leek, washed well and sliced
3 cloves garlic, finely sliced
few stalks of fresh thyme (optional)
500ml low-salt chicken stock
1 litre water
½ cup pearl barley
1½ cups cooked chickpeas (or 400g can chickpeas,
   drained and rinsed)
3 stalks celery, chopped (optional)
200g mushrooms, chopped (optional)
1 teaspoon sea salt
freshly ground black pepper
4 tablespoons fresh lemon juice
small handful of parsley, chopped

Heat olive oil in a large heavy-based saucepan over medium heat. Sauté onion until softened slightly.

Add diced chicken, leek, garlic and thyme, if using, and cook for about 10 minutes, stirring occasionally.

Add chicken stock, water, pearl barley, chickpeas and celery and mushroom, if using. Bring slowly to a boil, then use a ladle to skim off any foam that appears. Reduce heat to maintain a gentle simmer. Cook for a further 45 minutes until barley is soft.

Add salt, pepper and lemon juice. Simmer for a few more minutes before serving. Garnish with chopped parsley.

SERVES 6

Beetroot and avocado soup

This simple raw soup may be part of a nutritious family meal, yet it is also beautiful and luscious enough to serve as a first course for an elegant dinner. In summer, this soup can be made in advance, refrigerated and served chilled. In winter, heat it in a small saucepan until just warm. Juicing a chunk of ginger along with the carrots and beetroot will add a warming zing to this soup, too.

2 cups fresh carrot and beetroot juice
   (from about 600g carrot and 300g beetroot)
1 large avocado
½ teaspoon salt
1cm piece of ginger (optional)
chopped herbs for garnish
olive oil for garnish

Place juice, avocado flesh and salt, along with ginger if desired, in a blender and process on high speed until smooth. Pour directly into individual bowls. Garnish with chopped herbs and olive oil.

SERVES 4

Drinking vegetable juice is an exceptional way to get plenty of nutrients, without taxing your digestive system. With the fibre removed, your body is able to assimilate a much higher proportion of nutrients available. Vegetable juice is better than fruit juice and supports liver detoxification – especially greens, such as spinach, parsley and celery. Carrot, kale, lemon and ginger are a favourite combination of ours and a real treat for the immune system!

Overleaf: Beetroot and avocado soup

Hearty miso soup

Traditional Japanese miso soup is a thin broth with two or three dainty garnishes. Miso soup can also be made chock-full of vegetables – like this recipe, which more closely resembles a stew.

¼ cup dried wakame
1 onion, sliced
fresh ginger slices
¼ small pumpkin (400g), peeled, deseeded
  and chopped into bite-sized chunks
2 cups cauliflower, cut in small florets
300g firm tofu, cut into cubes
3 tablespoons miso (more or less)
1 spring onion, sliced

Soak wakame in 2 cups of water for 10–15 minutes. Bring 1.5 litres water to boil in a large saucepan. Add onion and ginger. Boil for several minutes. Add pumpkin, then lower heat to bring soup to a gentle simmer. Cook for 10 minutes. Drain wakame. Add cauliflower, tofu and wakame to soup. Simmer until the cauliflower is cooked.

Keep soup over a low heat. Place about 2 tablespoons of miso in a small sieve and partially immerse in soup. Using the back of a spoon, press miso through sieve so it dissolves into soup. Ideally, it will have a very slight salty taste that isn't too strong – the dominant flavour should be the sweetness from the vegetables. Add more miso if required and simmer for a minute or so longer.

Serve in individual bowls, garnished with sliced spring onion.

SERVES 4

Miso may also be used to add flavour to stews, noodle dishes, sauces and dressings. Mixed with tahini, miso makes a tasty spread for toast. Miso is a rich source of trace minerals, such as zinc, iron and copper, and also provides live enzymes which support intestinal health.

Pea and parsnip soup

An alternative name for this sweet and brightly coloured soup is Give Peas a Chance. The miso adds depth to the flavour plus a host of nutritional benefits. Alternatively, season the soup with sea salt.

2 tablespoons olive oil
1 large onion, chopped
500g parsnips, peeled and chopped
4 cups water
1½ teaspoons dried mint (or ⅓ cup fresh mint
  leaves, finely chopped)
500g frozen peas
2 tablespoons white miso
4 tablespoons natural yoghurt
extra mint for garnish

Heat olive oil in a large heavy-based saucepan over medium heat. Sauté onion until softened slightly.

Add parsnip and turn heat down low. Sauté parsnip for 10–15 minutes, stirring occasionally.

Add water and mint, bring to a boil and simmer over low heat for 15 minutes. Add frozen peas, bring soup back to a boil and simmer for 5 minutes.

Remove from heat and add miso.

Purée soup with a stick blender, or in a food processor. Check seasoning and adjust with miso, or sea salt if using.

Serve garnished with a swirl of yoghurt and a sprinkle of chopped fresh mint.

SERVES 4

Tomato and coconut soup with fish dumplings

A colourful, nourishing soup that warms the heart and belly, this is a genuine meal in a bowl! Add calamari, scallops or prawns if available.

SOUP
2 tablespoons peanut or rice bran oil
1 onion, sliced
1 tablespoon red curry paste
⅓ cup long-grain rice
400g can chopped tomatoes
1 teaspoon turmeric
2 cups water
400ml can coconut cream
juice of 1 lemon
1 teaspoon sea salt
chopped fresh coriander for garnish

DUMPLINGS
400g fresh, boneless, white-fleshed fish
1 egg
1 teaspoon fennel seeds, toasted (or 1 teaspoon ground cumin)
small bunch coriander, chopped
½ teaspoon salt

Heat oil in a large heavy-based saucepan over medium heat. Sauté onion until softened slightly.

Add red curry paste and rice. Cook for several minutes. Add tomato, turmeric and water. Bring to a boil and simmer for about 15 minutes.

Meanwhile, make fish dumplings. Cut fish into small chunks and place in a food processor fitted with an S blade.

Add remaining ingredients and process for 20–30 seconds until well combined.

When rice in soup is well cooked, add coconut cream. Bring to a low boil. Using a dessertspoon, scoop some of the fish mixture, squeeze it gently in the hand to form a dumpling and add to soup. They can be any shape but a consistent size is best. Continue making dumplings, adding to soup as you go, until all the fish mixture is used up. Add lemon juice and sea salt. Simmer for about 5 minutes until dumplings are just cooked.

Serve in individual bowls, garnished with coriander.

SERVES 4–6

Vegetables & salads

❊❊❊❊❊❊❊

*One of the first meals Anna made for me featured a salad of purslane –
a weed that was growing in the middle of her driveway! This lunch was
my introduction to the world of edible wild plants and confirmation
that I had, indeed, met a remarkable woman.* - **ROGER**

If we had to simplify the message of this book down to just three words, this is what we would say: Eat more vegetables!

Vegetables are generally low in calories and fats, but high in fibre, vitamins and minerals. Numerous studies have shown that increased consumption of vegetables improves health and longevity, lowering the risk of major diseases, such as cancer, heart disease, stroke, diabetes, arthritis and nervous-system disorders.

Eating 9–10 serves per day would put you in the top 10 per cent for vegetable and fruit consumption and you would be at lowest risk for degenerative diseases. That may seem like a lot, but it's easy to add vegetables to almost any meal. For example, serve steamed greens and mushrooms with poached eggs for breakfast, include a salad with lunch, and add plenty of diced vegetables and herbs to casseroles for dinner. Even snacks can be freshened up with crunchy sprouts, cucumber, carrot and celery.

EAT WITH THE SEASONS

Choosing to eat fruit and vegetables when they are in season will not only be good for your household budget, it will also ensure you're eating the best-quality, tastiest, freshest produce all year round. For instance, vine-ripened summer tomatoes are infinitely superior to glasshouse tomatoes in winter.

Cooking with the rhythms of the garden will make you appreciate foods with a limited growing season. You will also minimise your carbon footprint by eating only locally produced seasonal fruit and vegetables.

EAT PLENTY OF LEAFY GREENS

Of the hundreds of vegetables available, leafy greens are particularly nutrient-rich yet low in calories. The darker green leaves, such as spinach, kale and Chinese greens, are especially nutritious. Regularly eating greens helps build and maintain strong bones, cleanse the blood, strengthen the heart and boost the immune system. They are also easy to digest in combination with other food.

EAT PLENTY OF NON-STARCHY VEGETABLES

Non-starchy vegetables are dense in micronutrients and low in carbohydrates. Recent public health promotions recommend that half the food on a dinner plate should be non-starchy vegetables.

Non-starchy vegetables (listed from lowest to highest carbohydrate value) include: bean sprouts, leafy greens (spinach, silverbeet, kale, bok choy, puha, watercress and rocket), herbs (parsley, coriander, basil, etc), celery, radishes, sea vegetables (nori, wakame, karengo), broccoli, cauliflower, cabbage (also as sauerkraut), mushrooms, avocado, cucumber, capsicums, zucchini, spring onions, asparagus, leeks, Brussels sprouts, snow peas, green beans, tomatoes, eggplant, fennel, onions and carrots. Starchy vegetables include corn, potatoes, sweet potatoes, yams, pumpkin, butternut, taro and cassava.

Eat more serves of non-starchy vegetables than starchy ones. A useful guide is to imagine your plate half-filled with non-starchy vegetables, quarter-filled with starchy vegetables or grains, and quarter-filled with a protein food.

Balsamic-roasted beetroot with goat's cheese and rocket

We buy a wonderful, locally produced, organic goat's-milk cheese from our local farmers' market and simply shave it fine for this salad. A soft creamy feta would also work well with the concentrated sweetness of the roasted beetroot.

6–8 small beetroots (500g)
olive oil
pinch of sea salt
1 tablespoon balsamic vinegar
300g rocket leaves (including flowers, if available), washed and drained
100–200g goat's cheese, finely shaved or cut into small cubes
extra virgin olive oil for drizzling

Place whole, unpeeled beets in a small saucepan, cover with cold water and bring to a boil. After about 15 or 20 minutes check whether they are soft right through by piercing them with a skewer or sharp knife. When soft, drain and allow to cool for 10 minutes. Under cold running water, peel beets using your fingers. The tough outer skins should just rub off, but if this isn't working, peel them with a small knife.

Heat oven to 190°C . Slice beets into bite-sized segments. Place in a roasting dish and toss with about 1 tablespoon of olive oil and a pinch of salt. Roast for about 15 minutes, turning segments once or twice, until they start to shrink and caramelise.

Remove dish from oven and immediately sprinkle with balsamic vinegar, tossing slices to coat evenly.

When cool, arrange on 4 individual plates with the rocket leaves and goat's cheese. Drizzle with a little extra virgin olive oil before serving.

SERVES 4

Bok choy stir-fry

Spicy white pepper highlights the earthy/sweet flavour of bok choy. This method works with other Chinese greens too, including gui larn and choi sum or any other variety with thick but tender stems.

1 bunch bok choy (about 400g)
1 teaspoon rice bran oil
½ teaspoon toasted sesame oil
small pinch of ground white pepper
2–3 teaspoons shoyu

Trim base off bok choy to separate leaves. Slice stalks and leaves into 3cm lengths. Wash thoroughly and drain in a colander.

Heat a wok or large frying pan over high heat. Add the oils. When the oils are very hot, add the bok choy. Keep heat high and stir for 2–3 minutes until greens and stems have wilted. (The water on the leaves should be sufficient to create enough steam and prevent burning, but you can add a little extra water if necessary.)

Season bok choy with pepper and shoyu, toss for another 30 seconds and transfer into a serving dish. Serve immediately.

SERVES 4 AS A SIDE DISH

Stir-frying requires fast intense heat. Moisture on the leaves creates steam which rapidly wilts the greens. For successful stir-frying, use an oil that can be safely heated, such as rice bran or sesame oil, and follow these simple steps:
1. Cut everything into even, small or thin pieces.
2. Heat the wok or frying pan before adding the oil, but do not let the oil smoke.
3. Keep the heat high. Unless cooking relatively small amounts, fry each vegetable (or meat or tofu) separately.
4. Keep cooked ingredients warm in a covered bowl. Mix together at the end and heat through briefly.
5. For an extra healthy stir-fry, add water to half-steam/half-fry the vegetables.
6. Season each batch of vegetables with a little salt. This will draw out moisture and add to the steaming effect. Add shoyu towards the end of the cooking process to prevent it burning.

Cauliflower mash

A light and flavourful alternative to mashed potatoes, this tastes best when the cauliflower is only just cooked through – perhaps even slightly underdone.

1 medium-sized cauliflower (800g with
   leaves removed)
3 tablespoons olive oil
rind and juice of 1 small lemon
½ teaspoon sea salt
ground pepper

Cut cauliflower into chunks. Remove only tough parts of stem. Put about 2cm of water in a large saucepan and bring to a boil. Add cauliflower and cover. Steam over a high heat for several minutes until cauliflower is only just cooked. Test by poking a piece of the stalk with a small sharp knife. (It should be easily pierced.)

Place drained, hot cauliflower in a food processor or high-speed blender. Add olive oil, lemon rind, juice and salt and process on high speed until smooth.

Season with salt and pepper and serve immediately.

SERVES 4–6 AS A SIDE DISH

To maximise nutrient retention in your produce, buy local, refrigerate if required and eat as soon as possible. Don't wash vegetables before putting in the refrigerator, as too much moisture can damage them and cause browning. Most green vegetables keep best stored loose in the vegetable-conditioning drawer in your refrigerator. This moderates humidity and sustains the crunch in green leaves for up to 5 days. Root vegetables store well in the refrigerator for 1–2 weeks. Store mushrooms in a paper bag in the refrigerator for up to 7 days.

Oven-baked savoury wedges

Appease that craving for deep-fried chips with these tasty wedges. Enjoy them with a bowl of guacamole, or serve with a green salad and grilled fish or organic steak. Alternatively, try using different herb and spice combinations, and kumara (sweet potato) instead of potato.

1½ teaspoons organic vegetable stock powder or
   ½ teaspoon sea salt
½ teaspoon ground cumin
1 teaspoon dried rosemary
½ teaspoon curry powder
4 medium-sized (500g) roasting potatoes
2 tablespoons rice bran oil

Preheat a large oven tray in oven preheated to 200°C.

Mix together stock powder or salt, cumin, rosemary and curry powder.

Scrub potatoes, leaving skin on. Slice into even-sized wedges and place in a large bowl.

Pour rice bran oil onto wedges and tumble with your hands. Sprinkle herb-spice mix over wedges and stir gently until evenly coated.

Spread wedges evenly on the preheated oven tray. Bake until crispy on the outside and soft on the inside (about 15–25 minutes).

SERVES 2–4

Potato varieties suitable for roasting include Agria, Ilam Hardy, Red Rascal and Desiree. We prefer to use Agria which are firm and well-flavoured and have an appealing golden colour when cooked.

Broccoli and cauliflower salad

Blanching the broccoli and cauliflower creates a beautiful bright salad that is easy to digest.

sea salt
300g broccoli, cut into bite-sized florets
300g cauliflower, cut into florets slightly smaller
   than the broccoli
2 tablespoons sesame seeds
150g mung bean sprouts
1 red capsicum, deseeded and thinly
   sliced (optional)
segments from 1 orange, all pith removed
   (optional)
Orange soy dressing (see page 76)

Bring a large saucepan of water to a boil and add a couple of teaspoons of salt.

Keep heat high and add broccoli and cauliflower. After several minutes test a piece. Drain when cooked but still firm and crunchy to bite.

Immediately transfer vegetables to a large bowl. Put the bowl in the sink and cover vegetables with cold water. Leave them in the water until they feel cool.

Put a small frying pan over a low heat and toast the sesame seeds until fragrant and lightly coloured.

Combine all ingredients in a bowl and dress with plenty of orange soy dressing. Transfer to a serving dish.

SERVES 6

Sweet and sour kumara with shiitake

Shiitake mushrooms have long been used in Chinese medicine for their immunity-enhancing properties. Combined with the gorgeous sweet and sour kumara (sweet potato), this dish makes the perfect accompaniment to meat or fish.

6 dried shiitake mushrooms (25g)
2 tablespoons rice or cider vinegar
3 tablespoons shoyu
2 tablespoons arrowroot
1 teaspoon sesame oil
1 medium red onion, sliced
400g can pineapple pieces in juice
1½ cups water, or chicken or vegetable stock
500g kumara, sliced in big chunks about
   0.5cm thick
honey for sweetness (optional)
spring onions, finely sliced for garnish (optional)

✸ Soak mushrooms in water for at least 2 hours.

Drain mushrooms. Remove stems (discard) and slice caps into strips.

Mix rice vinegar, shoyu and arrowroot together in a small bowl.

Heat sesame oil in a large wide frying pan. Add mushroom and sauté for 2–3 minutes.

Add red onion and sauté for 1–2 minutes further.

Add pineapple pieces with juice. Add water or stock.

Arrange kumara slices on top. Cover the pan and boil hard for about 5–7 minutes until kumara is cooked through.

Turn heat down very low. Stir the vinegar/soy/arrowroot mixture and add to the pan. Stir everything immediately, as the sauce will quickly thicken. (Add honey for a sweeter taste if required.) Continue to cook on low heat, while gently stirring for 2 more minutes. Serve immediately garnished with the spring onions.

SERVES 6 AS A SIDE DISH

Shiitake are not only a delectable addition to Asian meals, they are also a dynamic healing food. Shiitake contain a powerful immunity-enhancing compound called lentinan that helps fight infection and also has anti-tumour properties. Soak shiitake mushrooms for at least 2 hours before adding to miso soup, noodle dishes and stir-fries.

Tempeh, corn and green bean salad

Some of these ingredients may be unfamiliar to you, but it's worth trying to find them to give this recipe a try. Salads are fun to play with, so if you can't find everything on the list, feel free to experiment. Canned corn works well too.

¼ cup arame (dried seaweed)
sea salt
1 cob fresh corn
150g fresh green beans, trimmed and cut in 3cm
  lengths
½ block tempeh (125g)
2 teaspoons rice bran oil
Umeboshi dressing (see page 76)

Cover arame with about 1 cup of water. Leave to soak while preparing other ingredients.

Bring a large saucepan of water to a boil and add a couple of teaspoons of salt. Keep the heat high and add the corn. When cooked but still firm and crunchy to bite, use a slotted spoon to lift corn from water and transfer it to a large bowl. Put bowl in the sink and cover corn with cold water. Leave it in the water until it feels cool.

Repeat with beans.

Drain cooled vegetables. Cut corn cob in half.

One at a time, stand corn halves on end on a chopping board, then slice off kernels using downward cuts, close to the core. Place corn in a bowl and use fingers to break apart the kernels.

Slice tempeh in half to make two thin, flat pieces.

Heat rice bran oil in a small frying pan over a moderate heat. Fry tempeh on each side until golden brown. When cool, slice into thin strips.

Drain arame and discard soaking water.

Mix corn, beans, tempeh and arame in a bowl. Add about 5 tablespoons of dressing to taste. Mix everything well and serve.

SERVES 4

Wild greens with sesame

Eating the fresh shoots of certain herbs stimulates the liver, helping to cleanse the body of toxins built up by rich winter food. This is an easy, delicious recipe that suits strong-tasting weeds such as sow thistle (puha), but also dark, leafy greens such as spinach, silverbeet or bok choy.

1 large bunch leafy greens
¼ cup freshly ground sesame seeds
1½ tablespoons shoyu

Two-thirds fill a large saucepan with water and bring to a boil.

Trim, wash and drain greens. Cut into 2–3cm lengths.

Drop greens into the boiling water and blanch briefly. (Most greens will need less than 1 minute.) Drain immediately.

When cool enough to handle, squeeze gently and transfer to a large bowl. Mix ground sesame seeds and shoyu with the greens. Check seasoning and adjust if necessary.

SERVES 4–6

Tempeh, corn and green bean salad

Kale and roasted pumpkin salad

Curly kale retains a good texture when cooked, holding its own in dishes where other greens would wilt into insignificance. Steamed kale has a wonderful earthy-green flavour that combines well with sweet pumpkin.

500g pumpkin, chopped into bite-sized chunks
2 tablespoons olive oil
½ teaspoon sea salt
several large kale leaves (250g)
2 tablespoons shoyu
8 Brazil nuts, chopped

Heat oven to 175°C.

Place pumpkin in a roasting dish with the olive oil and salt. Mix well. Roast for 20 minutes or until just cooked.

Wash and drain kale leaves. Strip leaves by hand, discarding hard stems. Chop leaves into large pieces.

Place kale in a saucepan with about 0.5cm water in the bottom, then cover. Steam over a high heat until softened. Remove from heat and drain off excess water.

Tip steamed kale onto roast pumpkin in roasting dish. Add shoyu and mix well.

Transfer vegetables into a serving dish and garnish with chopped nuts.

SERVES 6

The beautiful curly leaves of kale provide more nutritional value for fewer calories than almost any food. Like broccoli, kale also belongs to the Brassica family, a group of vegetables that has gained recent widespread attention due to their health-promoting and cancer-preventing phytochemicals. Kale is an excellent source of calcium and vitamin C. Just 1 cup supplies almost 90 per cent of the recommended daily intake for vitamin C. Try kale steamed and mashed into potato Dutch style, with gravy and sausages, or use in soups, stews and stir-fries.

Spinach salad with walnut pesto dressing

3 packed cups spinach leaves, washed and drained
½ cup walnuts, pine nuts or cashew pieces
1 cup basil leaves
4 tablespoons olive oil
1 tablespoon lemon juice
1–2 cloves garlic, roughly chopped
½ teaspoon sea salt
freshly ground black pepper

Chop the spinach leaves and stems into bite-sized pieces and place in a large bowl.

Place all remaining ingredients in a food processor. Pulse for 20–30 seconds until well combined but keeping some of the nuts fairly chunky.

Add to the spinach and mix by hand, ensuring all the leaves are well-coated.

Serve immediately.

SERVES 4

Kale and roasted pumpkin salad

Zucchini and olive pasta sauce

Zucchini grow like crazy over summer – sometimes they just can't be picked fast enough! When plump and cheap, use them as the base for this super-quick pasta sauce. To serve, simply pour the blended sauce onto cooked pasta and add the sliced olives. Top with feta or parmesan cheese.

400g zucchini, chopped into rough chunks
¼ red onion, chopped
1 tablespoon tomato paste
¼ cup olive oil
1 tablespoon organic powdered vegetable stock
1 tablespoon lemon juice
freshly ground black pepper
⅓ cup pitted kalamata olives, sliced

Place all ingredients except the sliced olives in food processor. Blend at high speed for 1–2 minutes until smooth.

Store in the refrigerator until required. Add olives just before serving.

SERVES 4

Roast Jerusalem artichokes

Jerusalem artichokes are easy to grow and delicious as part of a winter meal. They can be eaten raw in a salad, boiled in water or roasted. Coconut oil and butter combine to give a wonderful nutty coat to this earthy vegetable.

1 kg Jerusalem artichokes
1 tablespoon butter, melted
1 tablespoon cold-pressed coconut oil
½ teaspoon sea salt
freshly ground black pepper

Heat oven to 180°C.

Carefully scrub artichokes, pulling bulbs apart to remove dirt.

With a small knife, remove any tough, dry or discoloured parts and discard. Chop remainder into bite-sized chunks. Place in a roasting tray and add the butter, coconut oil, salt and pepper.

Place dish in oven. After 10 minutes, give artichokes a good stir to coat with melted oils and seasoning.

Bake for a further 20 minutes or so until artichokes are soft inside.

SERVES 4

Fresh vegetables and fruit straight from the garden or farmers' market are best, but for variety and convenience we occasionally buy frozen berries and vegetables. Although there is loss of nutrients in the freezing process, fresh produce in the supermarket has also suffered degradation during transport and in storage. At least frozen foods have been picked and packed at peak quality. Frozen vegetables require minimal cooking because they have been blanched briefly before packing.

Cabbage and bacon stir-fry

Steaming or stir-frying brings out the best in cabbage. The trick is to cook it hot and quick, adding the minimum amount of liquid, so it remains slightly crunchy.

100g free-range shoulder or middle bacon, cut into
  small slices
1 teaspoon fennel seeds
1 medium-sized onion, cut into long strips
300g cabbage, cut into bite-sized pieces
¼ cup white wine
½ teaspoon sea salt

Place a large, deep frying pan over a low-medium heat and sauté bacon and fennel seeds for 1-2 minutes until the bacon releases a little fat.

Add onion and sauté for several minutes further until softened.

Add cabbage, white wine and salt and give everything a good stir. Cover pan with a lid and turn up heat to medium-high. After 3 or 4 minutes stir again and check liquid. Add a little water if necessary. Continue to cook until cabbage is softened, but still slightly crunchy.

Serve immediately.

SERVES 4

Mango and avocado salsa

The tropical combination of mango and avocado is a party on a plate, brightening even the dreariest mood. This salsa can be served atop pan-fried fish or grilled chicken, or rolled up with feta and salad leaves for a lunchtime wrap.

1 avocado
1 mango
small handful of fresh mint, finely sliced
½ small red onion, finely sliced
2 tablespoons olive oil
juice of 1 lemon
½ teaspoon sea salt
freshly ground black pepper

Remove flesh from avocado and mango. Cut into small cubes and put in a bowl.

Add mint, red onion, olive oil, lemon juice, salt and pepper and mix gently to combine.

SERVES 4

Pear and walnut salad

Freshly shelled walnuts give a big lift to this salad. The pears need to be ripe but firm. Locally grown, shelled walnuts are now available in many supermarkets. For a well-balanced lunch, add a large slice of grilled haloumi cheese.

½ frilly green lettuce or 3–4 cups salad leaf mix
small bunch red radishes, trimmed and sliced into wedges
1–2 spring onions, finely sliced
2–3 pears, quartered, cored and sliced
½ cup (75g) walnuts, chopped into large pieces
Toasted sesame dressing (see page 76)

Wash lettuce leaves in plenty of water. Dry in a salad spinner or drain well. Tear into bite-sized pieces.

Place lettuce leaves, radish, spring onion, pear and walnut pieces in a large bowl.

To serve, add several tablespoons of dressing and gently toss to coat.

SERVES 4

Bulk-bin walnut pieces are generally slightly rancid and may have a bitter flavour. This can be improved by soaking them. Place the walnut pieces in a bowl, cover with cold water and add juice of half a lemon. After a couple of hours, drain and rinse before adding to the salad.

Asparagus and mushroom salad

Marinating the mushrooms in the dressing gives them a luscious silky texture, providing a lovely contrast to the crunchy raw asparagus and radishes. When asparagus is not in season try using blanched green beans or raw courgettes.

DRESSING
1 tablespoon lemon juice
1 tablespoon cider vinegar
2 teaspoons wholegrain mustard
¼ cup olive oil
½ teaspoon sea salt
ground black pepper

SALAD
1 bunch watercress
250g asparagus, trimmed
2–3 red radishes, trimmed
150g white button mushrooms, thinly sliced
roasted seeds (optional)
shaved sheep's feta (optional)

☀ Combine dressing ingredients in a small bowl and whisk together. Place mushrooms in a bowl, pour on dressing and mix well. Leave to marinate overnight, or, if pushed for time, for as long as it takes you to prepare the rest of the salad.

Pick through watercress, removing any tough stems. Wash and drain in a salad spinner. Arrange picked watercress in a flat serving bowl. Slice asparagus on the diagonal, long and thin. Slice in half lengthwise, then in thin pieces.

Add sliced asparagus and radishes to the mushrooms. Toss to combine. Spread salad on top of watercress. Garnish with roasted seeds or shaved feta, if using.

SERVES 4

It's easy to consume plenty of salad greens in summer, but in winter, when we are more inclined to eat heavier, richer, cooked foods, it is especially important to remember to eat a proportion of raw and lightly cooked greens. There are many green vegetables available through the winter months, such as kale, broccoli and Chinese greens.

Cauliflower salad with anchovy dressing

Anchovy fans will love this salad. Cauliflower is a good match for the rich dressing, which is loaded with healthy fats. It's great for lunchboxes and keeps well in the refrigerator for up to 3 days. If anchovies are not popular, use sun-dried tomatoes instead.

1 medium-sized cauliflower, cut into bite-sized florets
⅓ cup olives
100g goat's feta, cut into small cubes
3 tablespoons capers
4 handfuls of leafy greens (spinach or mesclun mix)

DRESSING
¼ cup olive oil
½ cup thick, natural yoghurt (Greek-style is best)
4 anchovies or sun-dried tomatoes
1–2 cloves garlic, sliced
2 tablespoons white balsamic vinegar
1 organic free-range egg

Put a large saucepan of salted water over a high heat and bring to a boil. Add cauliflower and cook briefly until just cooked but still a bit crunchy. Pour into a colander, cool under cold running water and leave to drain.

Put dressing ingredients in a small blender and process until smooth.

In a large bowl, combine cauliflower, olives, feta and capers. Pour dressing on top and mix well. Leave to marinate for at least 20 minutes, if time allows.

When ready to serve, add leafy greens and toss gently.

SERVES 4–6

Wakame cucumber salad with ponzu

Ponzu sauce is a simple, oil-free dressing that also makes a zesty dipping sauce for grilled fish and other seafood.

⅓ cup wakame
⅓ telegraph cucumber, cut into quarters lengthwise, deseeded and finely sliced
½ teaspoon sea salt

PONZU SAUCE
1 tablespoon lemon juice
1 tablespoon shoyu
2 tablespoons rice wine or cider vinegar

Soak wakame for 20 minutes in cold water.

Drain wakame, and if not already cut fine, remove any hard stems and chop leaves into small pieces.

Place cucumber in a bowl and rub in the salt. Leave for 15 minutes and squeeze out excess moisture.

Combine drained wakame and cucumber in a bowl.

Put sauce ingredients in another bowl and stir to combine.

SERVES 4 AS A SMALL SIDE DISH

Wakame is an edible seaweed that can be purchased in several forms. The easiest to use is fueru wakame, which has no hard stems and is already cut into little pieces. Most large supermarkets and Asian stores now stock this product.

Soba and watercress salad

This easy and substantial side dish pairs well with a simple piece of grilled fish.

250g packet soba noodles
¼ cup extra virgin olive oil
1½ tablespoons umeboshi vinegar
1–2 oranges, peeled and sliced
1 bunch watercress or rocket leaves

Cook soba noodles according to instructions on packet. Check regularly by pulling out a strand. When only just cooked, drain and rinse under cold running water.

In a large bowl, whisk olive oil and umeboshi vinegar together. Add noodles and orange pieces, then use your hands to coat everything evenly.

Pick through watercress, removing any tough stems. Chop into 6-7cm lengths. Wash in plenty of water and drain well.

Just before serving, add watercress to bowl and toss gently to combine.

SERVES 4

Soba noodles are usually made from a mixture of buckwheat and wheat flour. Pure buckwheat noodles are available from most organic suppliers for people with a wheat intolerance.

Umeboshi vinegar is salty and sour, made from Japanese pickled plums. If unavailable, substitute a mixture of red wine, vinegar and sea salt to taste.

Red radish pickles

These brightly coloured pickles keep for weeks in the refrigerator. They come in handy as a cheerful garnish for a salad or snack.

100ml red wine vinegar
1½ teaspoons sea salt
100ml water
1 bunch red radishes

Put vinegar, salt and water in a 375g jar. Cover and shake well to dissolve the salt.

Wash radishes and trim off tops and tails. Halve each radish, then slice as thinly as possible.

Pack radish slices into the jar. There needs to be just enough liquid to cover radishes when they are packed down. Add more vinegar if required.

Cover and refrigerate. Leave for at least 1 week before eating.

MAKES 1 JAR

Simple pressed salad

Salting and pressing makes vegetables more digestible, breaking down the cell structure without losing valuable food enzymes (as would happen if we cooked it). This method can be used for a large variety of vegetables, but works particularly well with cabbages.

500g red or green cabbage (or a mixture), finely sliced
2 teaspoons sea salt
300g pumpkin or carrot, peeled and grated
6 red radishes, finely sliced
1 bunch rocket (or other salad greens)
olive oil (optional, to dress)
vinegar (optional, to dress)

Place cabbage in a large bowl and rub in 1 teaspoon of salt. The cabbage will become glossy and moist as the salt begins to draw out moisture. Transfer to a smaller bowl, pack the cabbage down and place a plate and a heavy weight on top.

Place pumpkin and radishes in another bowl and rub in remaining salt. Place a plate and a heavy weight on top.

Leave everything to pickle for 2–3 hours.

When ready to eat, drain off any excess liquid and either mix the vegetables and rocket together or arrange side by side in a bowl.

Serve as is or lightly dressed with a little olive oil and vinegar.

SERVES 6 WITH LEFTOVERS FOR THE REST OF THE WEEK

Korean kimchi salad

Here's another light, clean-tasting salad that keeps well for several days. Salting the vegetables helps with digestion and also retards spoiling when not refrigerated. This is a perfect salad for a picnic!

1 small Chinese cabbage (500g), finely sliced
½ cucumber, cut into quarters lengthwise, deseeded and finely sliced
1½ teaspoon sea salt
2 garlic cloves, finely chopped
2cm piece of fresh ginger, finely sliced, minced or grated
1 fresh red chilli, seeds removed, finely chopped
1 red capsicum, deseeded and sliced
1 carrot, finely sliced or grated
2 tablespoon cider vinegar

Place cabbage and cucumber in a large bowl and rub with sea salt. The vegetables will start to go glossy as the salt draws out moisture. Leave for 15 minutes while preparing remaining ingredients.

Place garlic, ginger, chilli, capsicum, carrot and cider vinegar in a separate bowl.

Drain cabbage and cucumber in a colander or sieve. Take handfuls of cabbage and cucumber, lightly squeeze to remove excess moisture and add to the other ingredients. Mix to combine.

SERVES 6 WITH LEFTOVERS FOR THE REST OF THE WEEK

Salt is vital for life, balancing electrolytes in blood and body tissue. We recommend using sea salt harvested from evaporated sea water. Sea salt contains a range of valuable minerals but lacks iodine, so be sure to eat plenty of seafood and sea vegetables for your necessary iodine intake. Unprocessed sea salt brings a more subtle, complex flavour to food.

The cheapest, most common cooking salts are refined – stripped of nutrients – and contain anti-caking agents. Most people consume too much refined salt from processed products, fast food and over-seasoning. This is a well recognised contributing factor to heart disease.

Korean kimchi salad

Fresh mustard

Use this as a substitute for wholegrain mustard in dressings and sauces. It will keep in the refrigerator for at least 2 months.

½ cup yellow mustard seeds
½ cup water
¼ cup apple cider vinegar
½ teaspoon sea salt
½ small apple, grated
1 tablespoon raw honey

☀ Soak mustard seeds in the water overnight. The seeds will absorb all the water.

Drain soaked mustard seeds. Place in a blender along with other ingredients. Blend until well combined.

MAKES 1 JAR

Toasted sesame dressing

¼ cup mild olive oil
2 teaspoons toasted sesame oil
2 teaspoons cider vinegar
1½ tablespoons shoyu

Put all ingredients in a small jar and shake well to combine before use.

MAKES ⅓ CUP

Umeboshi dressing

½ cup olive oil
2 tablespoons umeboshi or red wine vinegar
1 tablespoon wholegrain mustard
1 clove garlic, chopped fine
black pepper

Put all ingredients in a small jar and shake well to combine before use.

MAKES ⅔ CUP

Orange soy dressing

juice of 2 oranges
½ cup olive oil
½ teaspoon mustard powder
2 cloves garlic, chopped
2 teaspoons honey
1½ tablespoons shoyu
1½ tablespoons cider vinegar

Put all ingredients in a small jar and shake well to combine before use.

MAKES ABOUT 1 CUP

Some oils are better than others. Here is the good oil from us:
* For salad dressings, dips and spreads use cold-pressed olive, flaxseed, walnut, avocado, and sunflower oils.
* For moderate-temperature cooking, such as baking and sautéeing, use olive oil, butter or coconut oil.
* For high-temperature cooking, such as pan-frying, stir-frying and roasting, use rice bran, sesame and coconut oil, or clarified butter (but only in small amounts).
* Please note that very high heat, for example when grilling and frying, may damage even the most stable cooking fats creating dangerous free-radicals.

Lemon tahini dressing

2 tablespoons lemon juice
1 tablespoon tahini
1 tablespoon honey
1 tablespoon Dijon mustard
½ cup olive oil
sea salt and freshly ground black pepper

Blend or whisk all ingredients together to form a thick, smooth consistency. Check seasoning and adjust, if required.

MAKES ABOUT ¾ CUP

Green goddess creamy dressing

½ avocado
½ orange with rind removed
¼ cup olive oil
1 tablespoon cider vinegar
½ cup chopped green herbs
1 teaspoon curry powder
sea salt and ground black pepper
water if necessary

Put avocado flesh and all other ingredients in a blender. Blend together until smooth. Adjust consistency with water.

MAKES 1½ CUPS

Apple ginger dressing

1 apple, cored and chopped
3 tablespoons olive oil
juice of 1 small lemon
1 teaspoon ginger powder
2 teaspoons cider vinegar
1 teaspoon wholegrain mustard
3 tablespoons water
½ teaspoon sea salt
ground black pepper (to taste)

Put all ingredients in a blender. Blend together until smooth.

MAKES 1 CUP

Polyunsaturated oils like nut and seed oils are fragile and degrade easily when exposed to heat and light. We recommend avoiding cheap oils from the supermarket, such as canola, safflower, soya and corn oil. They are highly processed and will cause oxidative damage to cells, speeding up the ageing process and contributing to disease.

Pulses
& grains

❀❀❀❀❀❀❀❀❀

Our enthusiasm for raw foods once led to a nasty run-in with kidney beans.
We sprouted them and ate a whole lot, resulting in explosive gas and stomach
cramps. We learnt the hard way that smaller pulses and seeds are best for sprouting
while the big ones, such as chickpeas and kidney beans, are best cooked. – ANNA

Pulses are the edible seeds of the legume family, including peas, beans and lentils. Regular consumption of pulses significantly increases life expectancy and positively benefits the digestive system and heart, while helping stabilise blood-sugar levels.

Grains come from the grass family. Whole grains provide plenty of starchy carbohydrates, minerals and vitamins for regular energy production.

Beans and whole grains are relatively inexpensive, easy to store and can be used in a variety of ways to form an important and tasty part of a healthy, balanced diet.

HERE ARE OUR TOP TIPS TO HELP YOU GET THE MOST FROM GRAINS:

❀ Eat whole grains. Processed grains like white rice and white flour have been stripped of the bran – the valuable outer layer.
❀ Soak whole grains for several hours or overnight before cooking. They will be quicker to cook and you'll end up with a creamier texture.
❀ Buy organically grown grains that are free from added chemicals.
❀ Use ancient wheat varieties, such as spelt and kamut. Avoid modern hybridised strains of wheat to minimise digestive problems.
❀ Reduce consumption of all flour products, including pasta. Enjoy cakes and pastries as occasional treats.

HOW TO COOK DRIED BEANS

1. Look for beans that appear plump and fairly uniform in size and colour. Remove any discoloured, broken, cracked or shrivelled beans as they won't cook properly.
2. Place beans in a large bowl, cover with water and soak overnight. (Only lentils and split peas can be cooked without prior soaking.)
3. Drain and rinse the soaked beans.
4. Place in a saucepan and cover with plenty of water – approximately 1 cup beans to 3 cups water. Do not add salt to the cooking water – this stops the beans from softening.
5. Bring to a rolling boil with the lid off and continue to boil rapidly.
6. Check occasionally and add more water if required – the beans need to be covered throughout the cooking process.
7. Continue to cook until the beans are soft.

HOW TO COOK WHOLE GRAINS

1. Rinse the grains briefly in a fine-mesh sieve under running cold water.
2. Transfer grains to a small saucepan. Add water (1 cup grains to 2 cups water) and sea salt.
3. Bring to a boil over medium heat and turn heat down very low.
4. Cover with a lid and simmer until all the water has been absorbed. Check all the water is gone by using a spoon to pull the grains aside at the bottom of the pot.
5. If time allows, fluff with a fork, cover and leave to stand for 10 minutes before serving.

COOKING TIMES (1 CUP GRAINS)

Adzuki beans	1 hour	Green lentils	30–45 minutes
Black beans	1–1½ hours	Red lentils	20–30 minutes
Fava beans	45–60 minutes	Puy lentils	20–30 minutes
Kidney beans	1–1½ hours	Amaranth	25–30 minutes
Lima beans	1–1½ hours	Barley	45 minutes
Mung beans	1–1½ hours	Brown rice	45 minutes
Pinto beans	1–1½ hours	Buckwheat	20 minutes
Soya beans	3 hours	Millet	20–25 minutes
Split peas	30–45 minutes	Quinoa	20 minutes
Chickpeas	1½–2½ hours		

For couscous, add a pinch of sea salt to 1 cup of water and bring to a boil. Add 1 cup of couscous, stir, cover and turn off heat. Leave for 5 minutes and then fluff couscous up with a fork.

A WARNING ABOUT WHEAT

Many people find they feel better after reducing their consumption of wheat. Some may have a wheat intolerance because they lack the enzymes needed to digest wheat proteins such as gluten efficiently. We personally recommend that everyone tries a two-week abstinence from all wheat products. There is a range of mild to severe health symptoms that can evaporate with this one simple dietary change.
Please note: people with coeliac disease are allergic to gluten and should cut it out of their diet forever.

Mexican chilli beans

These beans make a quick lunch on their own or may be served wrapped in a tortilla, with a bowl of corn chips, or poured over a baked potato. Ring the changes further with a wide range of accompaniments.

1 tablespoon olive oil
1 onion, diced
2 cloves garlic, minced
½ red capsicum, deseeded and chopped
1½ cups or 400g can cooked kidney beans or black beans
2 cups chopped fresh tomatoes or 400g can chopped tomatoes
1 teaspoon ground cumin
1 teaspoon dried oregano
1 teaspoon paprika
pinch of cayenne pepper (more or less)
½ teaspoon sea salt

Heat oil in a large, heavy-based frying pan.

Add onion and sauté for several minutes until starting to soften.

Add garlic and capsicum and sauté for 1 minute more.

Add all remaining ingredients. Bring to a boil and turn heat down low. Cover saucepan with a lid and simmer for 20-30 minutes.

Serve accompanied by any or all of the following: sour cream, diced avocado, sliced tomato, fresh salsa, chopped fresh coriander and/or sliced jalapeño peppers.

SERVES 4 AS A SIDE DISH

Tempeh and kumara curry

The nutty flavour and chewy texture of the tempeh combined with the creaminess of the kumara (sweet potato) work well in this dish. The vegetables can be varied according to the season. If you're not a fan of tempeh, try an extra cup of cooked chickpeas instead.

1 tablespoon rice bran oil
2 medium-sized onions, chopped
1 teaspoon cumin seeds
2cm piece fresh ginger, minced
1-2 tablespoons Thai red curry paste
½ cup water
200g carrots (or daikon)
500g kumara (or pumpkin), chopped into chunks
2 cups cooked chickpeas
400g block tempeh, cubed
1 tablespoon shoyu
½ teaspoon sea salt
400g can coconut milk
2 tablespoons tamarind paste or 1 tablespoon lemon juice
fresh chopped coriander or sliced spring onions to garnish

Heat oil in a large, heavy-based saucepan.

Add onion and cumin and sauté for several minutes.

Add ginger and curry paste (be cautious if using a hot variety) and sauté for 1 minute further.

Add water, carrot (or daikon), pumpkin (or kumara), chickpeas, tempeh, shoyu, salt and coconut milk, and bring to a boil.
Turn the heat down low. Cover and cook for 30 minutes or until vegetables are very soft.

Add tamarind paste (or lemon juice) and gently mix the curry.

Serve garnished with coriander or sliced spring onion with brown or basmati rice.

SERVES 4

Tempeh is one of the most nutritious ways to eat soya beans. Try grilled tempeh with satay sauce in a burger, or crumbled up into a bolognaise sauce instead of mince.

Pressure-cooked brown rice

Pressure cookers are not as common as they once were but perhaps, as the world becomes more energy-conscious, they will make a comeback. They are both time and energy efficient. We use ours regularly for cooking everything, but find it is especially good for cooking brown rice.

Cooked under pressure, brown rice becomes satisfyingly rich and full tasting, with a wonderful sticky texture. The cooked rice keeps well in the refrigerator and we always cook enough for at least two meals. You will need to begin cooking it about 1½ hours before serving time.

1½ cups brown rice
2 cups water
pinch of sea salt

Wash rice thoroughly in a fine-mesh sieve under cold running water.

Put rice, water and salt in the pressure cooker. Secure lid. Place over medium heat and bring gradually up to pressure. When there is a good strong hiss of steam from the cooker, turn heat down low. Adjust heat to maintain pressure – a steady gentle hiss. Cook for 40 minutes.

Turn off heat and allow rice to cool. Once pressure has dropped enough to open cooker, gently mix rice with a wooden spoon before serving.

(For a variation, add ⅓ cup soaked dried soya beans, chickpeas or adzuki beans, or 1 cup chopped kumara or pumpkin to the cooker with the rice. No extra water is required.)

SERVES 6

Millet with pumpkin and nori

Novice seaweed-eaters can reduce the amount of nori or use freshly chopped parsley and garlic instead.

1 cup millet
2 cups water
½ teaspoon sea salt
2 sheets nori seaweed
1½ cups (200g) pumpkin, peeled, deseeded and
  cut into bite-sized pieces
Tamari roasted seeds (see page 42)

Wash millet in a fine-mesh sieve under cold running water. Put millet in a saucepan with water and salt.

Cut nori sheets into small pieces with scissors and sprinkle evenly on top of the water. Spread pumpkin on top of the nori and cover saucepan with a lid.

Bring to a boil, then turn heat down very low. Leave to simmer for about 20 minutes until all the water has been absorbed.

Turn off heat and leave to stand for a few more minutes. Mix gently with a wooden spoon before serving.

Serve sprinkled with *Tamari roasted seeds*.

SERVES 4

A pressure cooker can turn dried beans and grains into fast food, reducing cooking time by more than one-third. Pressure-cook large beans like chickpeas and kidney beans for 15–20 minutes. Smaller pulses, like lentils or mung beans, will cook in 10 minutes or less.

Gado-gado

This exotic-tasting dish is a well-balanced and satisfying meal. To avoid cooking, try making the salad with sliced tomatoes and cucumbers instead of beans or broccoli and carrots.

4 free-range organic eggs
150g green beans or broccoli, cut into
   bite-sized florets
250g carrots, cut into batons
150g cabbage, sliced
½ red capsicum, deseeded and sliced
100g mung bean sprouts
200g tempeh or tofu, sliced into rectangular
   strips about 0.5cm thick
Satay sauce (see below)

Hard-boil the eggs. (It will take about 8 minutes from when they come to a boil.)

In a separate saucepan of boiling salted water, blanch green beans and carrots in two separate batches.

Mix blanched green beans and carrots with the cabbage, capsicum and mung bean sprouts.

Pan-fry tempeh or tofu slices in a little coconut or sesame oil until golden. Slice when cool.

Peel and cut eggs in quarters lengthwise.

Divide mixed vegetables between 4 individual plates. On top of each, arrange tofu slices and egg quarters. Drizzle on plenty of *Satay sauce*, served warm or at room temperature.

SERVES 4

We usually have sprouts in the refrigerator where they will keep for a week or so. Our favourites are lentils and mung beans. Here's how to sprout beans:

1. SORT: Check the beans before use and remove any obviously malformed or discoloured beans.
2. SOAK: Place beans in a bowl and cover with plenty of water. Leave overnight.
3. DRAIN: Rinse sprouts at least once a day and drain thoroughly.
4. EAT: As a general rule, wait until the sprout tail is about as long as the seed itself. When the tips of the sprouts are starting to go green, transfer them to an airtight container and store in the refrigerator.

Satay sauce

Our version of satay sauce is made simply in a blender without cooking. In addition to its starring role in *Gado-gado*, try serving it over grilled fish or with chicken skewers.

1 tablespoon red curry paste (more or less)
100ml coconut milk
1 tablespoon shoyu
1 tablespoon lemon juice
4 tablespoons (60g) peanut butter
2 tablespoons grated palm sugar or
   whole cane sugar

Put all ingredients in a blender and process until smooth.

Adjust seasoning to taste. Add more curry paste if you want extra spiciness.

MAKES 1 CUP

Some nutritionists believe soy products are a wonderful source of low-fat protein while others consider them unsuitable due to high levels of substances that interfere with protein digestion. However, proper fermentation prevents this problem. We recommend you minimise your intake of unfermented soy products, such as tofu and soy milk, and products with added soy protein. Fermented soy products, including tamari, miso, natto and tempeh, can be safely consumed on a regular basis. Cheaper brands of shoyu are not fermented – check labels carefully before buying.

Gado-gado

Buckwheat kasha

Here is a traditional Slavic method of preparing buckwheat. The chicken stock makes this a robust and nutritious dish. If you use water instead of stock you will need to add sea salt.

1 cup buckwheat
1 egg, lightly beaten
2 cups chicken or vegetable stock or water
2 tablespoons butter or olive oil
freshly ground black pepper to taste
sea salt to taste
1–2 spring onions, finely sliced

Heat a heavy-based saucepan over medium heat and add buckwheat. Toast buckwheat, stirring often with a wooden spoon, for 3-4 minutes until fragrant and slightly browned. Remove pan from heat and leave to cool for at least 5 minutes.

Pour egg onto buckwheat in the pan. Return to heat and stir constantly until egg is cooked but grains are separated. This may happen very quickly if pan is still quite warm!

Add stock and butter and season with pepper and salt. Bring to a boil, cover and cook for 20-25 minutes.

Leave to cool for 10 minutes then gently fold in the spring onion.

Serve immediately with a salad for lunch or as part of a main meal.

SERVES 4

Almond pilaf

Pilaf is a traditional Middle-Eastern rice dish, flavoured with aromatic spices. In some cultures, pilaf is baked in an oven. However, this version can be quickly assembled and cooked on the stovetop, using the same absorption method as for steamed rice.

2 tablespoons olive oil or clarified butter
1 onion, finely diced
½ teaspoon fennel seeds
1 cup basmati rice
1 teaspoon ground cinnamon
1 tablespoon vegetable stock powder
¼ cup almonds, chopped
2 cups cold water

Put oil or butter in a saucepan over moderate heat. When butter has melted, add onion and fennel seeds and sauté until onion is soft.

Add remaining ingredients to pan, including water, and cover. Bring to a boil and turn heat down low. Simmer for 15-20 minutes.

Turn heat off and leave pilaf to stand for about 10 minutes. Mix gently with a wooden spoon before serving.

SERVES 6

Be careful when it comes to storing and eating leftover foods, particularly grains and meats. Cool and refrigerate or freeze in clean containers as soon as possible after dinner. Cooked grains in particular can quickly attract yeast and bacteria, so eat within 2 days.

Almond pilaf

Red quinoa salad with pears and feta

Red quinoa - although more maroon than red - has all the wonderful nutritional properties of regular quinoa and a dramatic bright colour. If preferred, use cow's feta or blue cheese instead of goat's feta. It will still be delicious.

1 cup quinoa
2 cups water
½ teaspoon sea salt
2 tablespoons sliced almonds
2–3 firm but ripe pears
2 tablespoons olive oil
lemon juice to taste
1 tablespoon fresh chives or spring onions, finely
   sliced
110g goat's feta

Rinse quinoa thoroughly in a fine-mesh strainer under cold running water, then drain.

Place quinoa in a large saucepan, add water and salt and bring to a boil. Cover and leave to simmer for about 15 minutes until all the water has been absorbed.

Toast sliced almonds in a small saucepan over low heat until just starting to colour.

Slice pears into quarters, remove core and slice flesh into long thin strips.

Place quinoa, pears, almonds, olive oil, lemon juice and chives or spring onions in a bowl and toss to combine.

To serve, crumble feta on top and gently mix to combine.

SERVES 6

Goat's feta is a staple ingredient in our household. Goat's milk and goat's milk products are beneficial because goat's milk:
* has a similar chemical structure to human milk
* is lower in fat and has much smaller fat molecules than cow's milk, making it easier to digest
* has been found to soothe problems in the digestive tract
* products are not mucus-forming
* is less allergenic than cow's milk.

Warm cannellini and spinach salad

Serve these creamy white beans and Mediterranean vegetables on toast for a nourishing lunch. Alternatively, use them as a base for grilled or pan-fried fish.

3 tablespoons extra virgin olive oil
1 large red onion, chopped
4 cloves garlic, minced
2 x 400g cans cannellini beans, drained
100g spinach leaves (small bunch), washed and
  roughly chopped
2 large tomatoes, chopped
zest and juice of 1 lemon
½ teaspoon sea salt
freshly ground black pepper
¼ cup chopped fresh parsley or basil

Heat a large saucepan on a moderate heat. Add olive oil, onions and garlic, and gently sauté until onions are starting to soften.

Add cannellini beans and heat through. Add spinach and tomatoes. Continue heating until the spinach wilts slightly. Remove from heat.

Add lemon juice and zest, salt, pepper and fresh herbs. Mix gently to combine. Serve immediately.

SERVES 6

Red lentil stew

Humble and often maligned, lentils are actually nutritional superstars! This simple stew has a wonderful earthy flavour, perfect for autumn and winter. Eat this dish on its own for lunch or with fish and greens for a hearty dinner.

2 cups brown or green lentils
1 tablespoon olive oil
1 onion, sliced
3 cloves garlic, chopped
2 carrots, roughly chopped
500g pumpkin, peeled, deseeded and
  roughly chopped
4 bay leaves
2 tablespoons miso
1½ teaspoons sea salt
ground black pepper to taste
small bunch parsley, chopped

☀ Soak lentils in water overnight.

Drain and rinse lentils, then set aside until required.

Heat a large heavy-based casserole dish over medium heat. Add oil, onion and garlic and sauté for a few minutes.

Add lentils, carrot, pumpkin and bay leaves. Cover with water to about 2cm above contents and bring to a boil.

Skim off any foam and turn heat down to maintain a low boil. After 20 minutes check that there is still sufficient water. (You want to have just a little liquid remaining after the lentils are cooked.) Continue cooking for 30 minutes or until lentils are soft.

Dissolve miso in a little of the liquid from stew and add to dish. Add sea salt and pepper.

To serve, mix in freshly chopped parsley.

SERVES 6–8

Pulses are an excellent source of dietary fibre, protein, B vitamins, iron, magnesium and several other important minerals. Look for beans that appear plump and fairly uniform in size and colour. There should be few, if any, cracked, broken or discoloured beans. Buy from a retailer that is likely to have a high turnover of stock to avoid buying old, over-dry beans that won't cook or sprout uniformly.

Warm cannellini and spinach salad

Lentil and grapefruit salad with mint dressing

Leftovers can result in strange and wonderful combinations, such as this salad that Anna created the day after a dinner party. Try it for lunch with a slice or two of fresh bread, or with grilled fish or chicken for a substantial dinner.

⅔ cup brown or green lentils
1 sweet grapefruit
2 large handfuls fresh salad greens (e.g. lettuce, rocket or spinach)
1 medium-sized avocado, cut into small cubes
1 small fennel bulb, core removed and finely sliced

DRESSING
50ml olive oil
1 tablespoon pomegranate molasses or honey
1 tablespoon cider vinegar
½ cup fresh mint leaves, chopped
½ teaspoon sea salt

Boil lentils in 4 cups of water for 20 minutes or until cooked. Drain and leave to cool.

Remove skin and white pith from outside of grapefruit. Cut into thin segments or slices, removing any seeds or tough core.

If salad greens have large leaves, chop into short lengths.

Place lentils, grapefruit, avocado, fennel and greens in a bowl.

To make the dressing, whisk ingredients together in a separate bowl.

When ready to serve, pour dressing over lentil salad and mix gently to combine.

SERVES 4

Adzuki pumpkin casserole

Dried adzuki beans look like small kidney beans and are available at health-food stores and some supermarkets. This is a good dish to eat regularly if you suffer from blood-sugar imbalances.

1 cup dried adzuki beans
1 tablespoon sesame or rice bran oil
1 large onion, chopped
2cm piece fresh ginger, sliced fine or grated
2½ cups water
800g pumpkin, peeled, deseeded and cut in bite-sized pieces
1½ tablespoons shoyu or 2 tablespoons miso
1 spring onion, finely sliced

☀ Soak adzuki beans in water overnight.

Drain and rinse adzuki beans.

Put oil in a large saucepan over medium heat and sauté onion until it begins to soften.

Add the ginger and cook for several more minutes. Add adzuki beans and water. On top of beans, spread pumpkin pieces. Finally, add shoyu or miso.

Bring to a boil, turn heat down to medium (beans need a fairly strong boil to cook properly) and cover.

Check after about 20 minutes that there is still plenty of liquid around the beans. After about 30 minutes of cooking, beans and pumpkin should be cooked.

Gently mix stew to combine and serve garnished with spring onions.

SERVES 4–6

Here are our best time-saving tips for using beans:
⊛ Cook a large batch of beans and freeze in several small containers – this works especially well for larger beans such as chickpeas and kidney beans. Thaw them in boiling water or add directly to soups or stews.
⊛ Canned beans are not as nutritious or tasty as home-cooked, but they are a handy standby when you are in a hurry. Always remember to rinse beans before use. Organic varieties are worth the small extra cost.

Seafood & meat

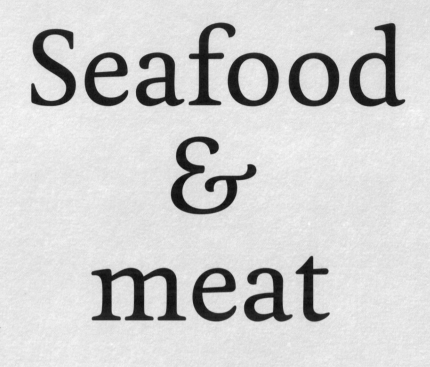

After being vegetarian for several years, one night I had a vivid dream about ravenously chomping on a leg of lamb, cave-woman style. This dream confirmed the growing sense that my body needed some animal protein . . . and it sure felt great to eat meat again! – ANNA

IS MEAT ESSENTIAL?

Over the years, we have each adopted vegan or vegetarian diets at different times and both have found that while a well-balanced vegan diet was cleansing and purifying, eventually it left us feeling under-nourished. However, we know that this is not everyone's experience. For instance, we know a great many healthy vegetarians and vegans who are enthusiastic and creative home cooks. These people make careful food choices to ensure they meet their essential daily protein and mineral requirements.

Provided non-meat-eaters include plenty of high-protein foods in their diet, such as pulses, grains, dairy or soy products, eggs, nuts and seeds, they should be fine.

While there are often complex cultural, social, ethical and ecological reasons behind people's food choices, ultimately we all need to respect each other's decisions.

SEAFOOD

Seafood is an easily digested form of protein and a good source of essential fatty acids. Consuming two or more servings of seafood per week has proven health benefits. Opt for fresh locally sourced fish as much as possible. Farmed salmon is readily available in most countries too. Fresh unprocessed seafood, such as whole fish and mussels, are, perhaps, the most affordable options.

Due to global environmental pollution, all fish contain small amounts of pesticide residue. Larger fish also accumulate heavy metals, such as mercury. However, most experts agree that the benefits of eating seafood outweigh the risks and careful choices can reduce exposure to toxic chemicals. To minimise the risk, eat only small amounts of large fish, such as tuna, swordfish and shark (lemon fish). Pregnant and breastfeeding women should completely avoid eating large fish.

MEAT

If you choose to eat meat, have small or moderate portions with plenty of non-starchy vegetables to fill the plate. Plant foods provide the nutrients and fibre that cleanse the body of toxic by-products from meat digestion. In particular, raw and fermented plant foods contribute to healthy intestines.

Eat meat from healthy animals that have been raised and killed humanely. This recommendation is as much for your own health and well-being as it is for the animals' welfare. Talk to suppliers and learn as much as possible about how meat has been produced before you buy.

Avoid using high temperatures to cook meat. Charring meat on a barbecue or in a hot frying pan creates carcinogenic compounds. Gentle cooking methods such as braising or stewing are preferable.

Lean game meats are now widely available in most countries. New Zealand beef and sheep are relatively healthy, grass-fed animals and locally produced organic beef and lamb meat is an even better option. Always choose free-range chicken and pork – aside from the ethical issues, the texture and taste of cage-free organic meat is vastly superior.

Indonesian fish cakes

Authentic South-East Asian food is alive with complex flavours from fresh herbs, spices and juices. For a shortcut, replace the fresh ginger, garlic and chilli with red curry paste – the fishcakes will still be tasty.

4 cloves garlic
2cm piece fresh ginger, sliced
½ fresh red or green chilli, chopped
3 tablespoons lemon juice
1 teaspoon cumin seeds
1 organic free-range egg
1½ tablespoons fish sauce
small bunch fresh coriander, chopped
600g fresh, boneless, white fish, roughly chopped
⅔ cup corn kernels or 100g green beans,
  finely chopped

Preheat oven to 180°C. Line a baking tray with baking paper.

Put garlic, ginger, chilli, lemon juice, cumin seeds, egg, fish sauce and coriander in a food processor and process for 30 seconds. Add chopped fish and process until mixture forms a sticky ball.

Transfer mixture to a bowl and mix in the corn kernels.

Form mixture into balls or flat rissoles about 1.5cm thick and place on prepared tray. Bake for 10–12 minutes until cooked through.

SERVES 4–6

Ceviche

This is the Spanish name for citrus-marinated fish. Versions of this dish are made in almost all tropical regions of the world, including the South Pacific. The most important consideration is that the fish is as fresh as possible.

400g fresh, firm white-fleshed fish
3 tablespoons lime juice or lemon juice
½ small red onion, finely diced
1 carrot, finely sliced or grated
½ red capsicum, deseeded and finely sliced
1 red chilli, deseeded and finely sliced
2 cloves garlic, minced
1 tablespoon fish sauce
1 cup coconut cream
sea salt
small bunch fresh coriander, roughly chopped

Slice fish into small, thin bite-sized pieces. Place in a bowl, add lime or lemon juice and mix well. Cover and leave in the refrigerator for at least 15 minutes or up to 2 hours.

To serve, combine marinated fish including juices with vegetables, chilli, garlic, fish sauce and coconut cream. Mix gently by hand.

Check seasoning and add a little salt if required.

Serve with steamed rice, avocado slices, salad leaves, taco shells or crackers.

These days most suppliers know how to provide good-quality fresh fish. As soon as you reach home, transfer the fish to a ceramic or glass container. Cover with cling film, store in the refrigerator and eat within 2 days.

Marinated grilled fish

Mild, white-fleshed fish readily absorbs the flavours of simple marinades in just a few minutes. Cooking fish under a grill is quicker, easier and less messy than pan-frying, especially when there are more than one or two people to serve.

150–200g fresh fish fillets per person
1 tablespoon your chosen marinade per person (see *Ginger shoyu marinade* and *Lemon garlic marinade* below and *Chermoula marinade* on next page)

Portion fish into pieces about 70–100g each, to make 2–3 pieces per serve. If possible slice fish so that portions are about the same thickness, so they cook evenly.

Place portioned fish in a bowl with the marinade. Toss gently until evenly coated. Leave for 10 minutes.

Heat grill.

Transfer fish to a shallow oven tray and place under grill.

Turn fish over after several minutes and continue grilling until cooked through.

If white liquid appears out of the top of the fish, it's cooked. With practice it is possible to remove the fish before this occurs and it will complete cooking with its own heat. (Underdone fish can still be moist and delicious. Overcooked fish is dry and tough.)

When cooking for large numbers, it can be easier to bake marinated fish in an oven preheated to 220°C. In that case, there's no need to turn each portion over halfway through cooking.

Ginger shoyu marinade

1 tablespoon finely grated fresh ginger or store-bought minced ginger
1½ tablespoons shoyu
2 tablespoons olive oil

Place the ingredients in a screw-top jar and shake to combine.

SERVES 4

Lemon garlic marinade

4 cloves garlic, finely chopped
1½ tablespoons lemon juice
2 tablespoons olive oil
½ teaspoon sea salt
chopped fresh or dried herbs (optional)

Place the ingredients in a screw-top jar and shake to combine.

SERVES 4

Chermoula marinade

This North African marinade can be easily made in a small blender, although the hand-chopped herbs have an appealing texture and appearance.

½ cup (packed) finely chopped fresh coriander
½ cup (packed) finely chopped Italian parsley
½ cup olive oil
2 tablespoons lemon juice
1 tablespoon ground cumin
2 tablespoons paprika
½ teaspoon cayenne pepper
4 cloves garlic, chopped
½ teaspoon sea salt

Put all the ingredients in a small bowl. Mix with a spoon to combine.

If it is too rich, add a little water or blend in a chopped fresh tomato.

Store leftover chermoula in the refrigerator for up to 2 weeks.

MAKES ABOUT 1 CUP

USE 2–3 TABLESPOONS TO SERVE 4

Pad Thai with calamari

Our version of this well-known Thai dish includes plenty of vegetables. Frozen calamari rings (without crumbs) are now available at most large supermarkets. Tempeh, tofu or prawns may be used instead of calamari.

150g Pad Thai rice noodles (thin, flat noodles)
1 tablespoon rice bran oil
2 eggs, lightly beaten
200g frozen calamari rings, defrosted and drained
½ cup finely sliced zucchini, red capsicum or carrot
250g mung bean sprouts
¼ cup cashews, roughly chopped
2 spring onions, sliced
small bunch fresh coriander

SAUCE
1 tablespoon tamarind paste or lemon juice
2 tablespoons fish sauce
1–2 teaspoons chilli sauce
2 teaspoons honey

Place rice noodles in a large bowl and cover with boiling water. Leave for about 7–10 minutes until soft. Drain.

Place sauce ingredients in a small bowl and whisk to combine.

Heat a wok or large frying pan and add 1 teaspoon of rice bran oil. Stir-fry the eggs until cooked through and broken into small pieces. Remove from wok and set aside until required. Clean wok if necessary.

Reheat wok and add 2 teaspoons rice bran oil. Gently stir-fry the calamari for about 2 minutes.

Turn heat up to medium–high and add zucchini, sprouts and cashews. Cook until sprouts are slightly softened.

Add sauce and rice noodles, then heat and stir until noodles are hot. If noodles begin to burn or stick to the pan, add a little water.

Turn heat down then add fried egg, spring onion and coriander. Mix well and serve immediately in individual bowls.

SERVES 2–3

Overleaf: Pad Thai with calamari

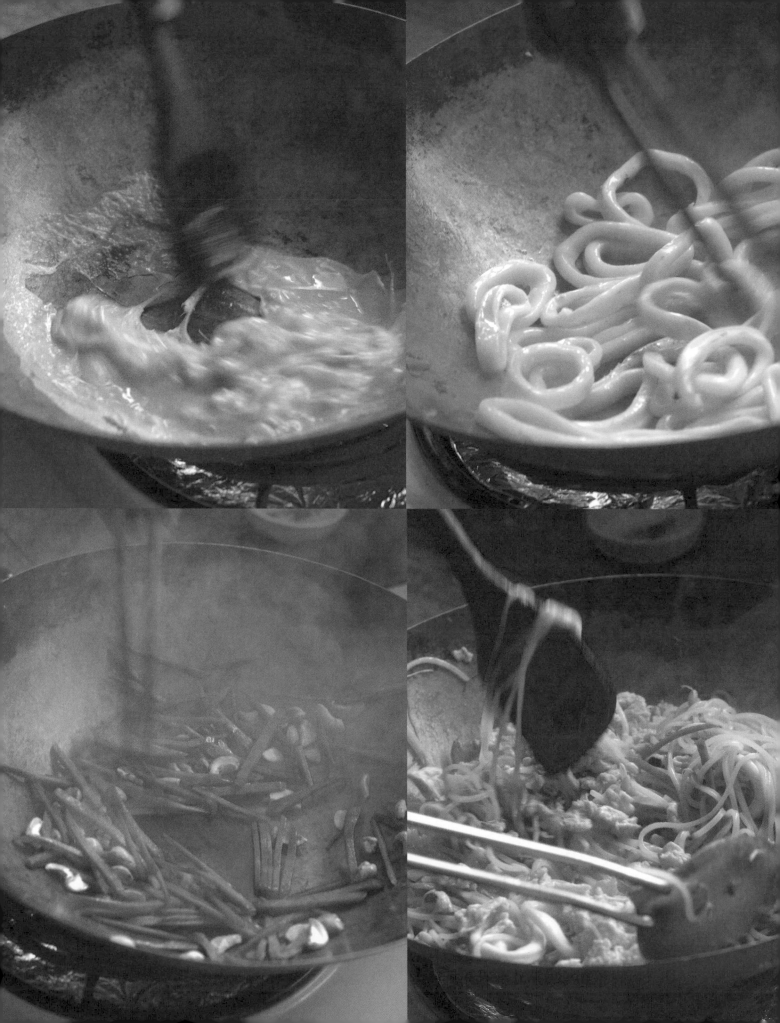

Smoked fish frittata

A rich, smoky aroma will fill the kitchen as this frittata slowly bakes.

small bunch silverbeet (400g), washed well
8 organic free-range eggs
200ml yoghurt
¼ teaspoon grated nutmeg
1 teaspoon sea salt
black pepper
3 medium-sized carrots (400g), grated
200g smoked fish, skin removed
½ red capsicum, deseeded and cut into strips
(optional)

Preheat oven to 160°C. Line with baking paper or lightly oil a 20 x 30cm baking dish.

Cut silverbeet stems and leaves into 2cm strips. Place in a saucepan with about 1cm of water. Cook over high heat for several minutes until spinach leaves have wilted. Drain and leave to cool.

Place eggs, yoghurt, nutmeg, salt and pepper in a bowl and whisk to combine.

Press grated carrot into prepared baking dish. Pour some egg mixture over carrot and press down through carrot. Add silverbeet in an even layer. Pour rest of egg mixture evenly over top of silverbeet.

Break smoked fish into small pieces and scatter over the top. Push fish down into egg mix a little. Arrange sliced capsicum on top if desired.

Bake for about 30-40 minutes until completely cooked. Check by giving the centre of the frittata a little press with your finger. The top will feel firm and appear lightly puffed up when it is ready. Leave to cool slightly before slicing and serving.

SERVES 6-8

Be creative with your frittata filling ingredients. Try hot smoked salmon and puha (sow thistle), blue cheese and grated pumpkin or feta, mushroom and spinach. Frittata keeps for 2 or 3 days in the refrigerator and packs easily for school, office, picnic or pot-luck parties. Cut into small squares, it can be served as a finger-food.

Gluten-free lasagne

Rice paper sheets are available from Asian supermarkets. However, some brands include wheat flour so check the ingredients list on the packet to make sure your lasagne is gluten-free, if necessary. Use this basic lasagne recipe and adapt the filling for the season.

LAMB LAYER
1 teaspoon rice bran oil
1 medium-sized onion, chopped
450g lamb mince
3 cloves garlic, minced
400g can tomatoes, chopped
3 tablespoons tomato paste
1 teaspoon sea salt
½ teaspoon black pepper
2 teaspoons Worcestershire sauce

GRILLED VEGETABLE LAYER
1 tablespoon rice bran oil
400g pumpkin or kumara (sweet potato), peeled
400g zucchini, red capsicums or mushrooms
½ teaspoon sea salt

LASAGNE
100g rice paper sheets (about 10 sheets)
2 egg yolks
2 cups yoghurt
grated Parmesan (optional)

Put oil and onion in a frying pan over medium heat and sauté until slightly softened.

Add lamb and garlic. Continue cooking until mince is browned, breaking up lumps with a wooden spoon.

Add tomatoes, tomato paste, salt, pepper and Worcestershire sauce. When boiling again, turn heat down, cover and simmer for 15–20 minutes. Remove from heat and allow to cool.

To prepare grilled vegetables, preheat oven to 180°C. Oil 2 baking trays.

Slice vegetables in 0.5cm-wide strips of even thickness and arrange on prepared trays. Season with salt. Bake about 15–20 minutes until just soft. Check as you may need to remove the softer vegetables early.

To assemble lasagne, oil a 20cm x 30cm ovenproof dish and lay the grilled vegetables evenly across the bottom.

Fill a large bowl with warm water. Put 2 sheets of rice paper in the water and soak for 30 seconds or until soft. Lift each sheet out carefully and lay on top of the vegetables. Repeat several times to create an even layer of rice paper 3–4 sheets thick. Pour lamb mixture on top. Create another layer of rice paper sheets.

Whisk egg yolks and yoghurt together in a small bowl and spread on top. Sprinkle with Parmesan, if using.

Bake in the middle of the oven at 180°C for 30 minutes or until starting to bubble at the edges.

Get into the habit of making one big main dish for your evening meal and serving a simple green salad alongside it. Casseroles, soups, stews and lasagne are ideal for this.

Wild venison rissoles

Oats and plenty of vegetables add fibre to these rissoles, making them deliciously soft and moist. While chopping ingredients by hand makes for an interesting texture, using a food processor can save time if you're in a hurry. As an alternative, use beef mince.

1 onion, finely chopped
350g carrot or parsnip, grated
½ cup parsley, finely chopped
½ cup rolled oats (ground fine if using whole grains)
2 teaspoons dried oregano
1 teaspoon paprika
½ teaspoon sea salt
pinch of black pepper or cayenne pepper
500g wild venison mince

Preheat oven to 180°C. Oil a roasting dish.

Put everything except the mince in a large bowl and mix well.

Add mince and mash with the hands and fingers until well combined.

Form mixture into patties or balls and place in prepared dish.

Bake for about 10-15 minutes until cooked through. (Cooking time will depend on the thickness of the rissoles.)

For a variation, pour chopped tomatoes or tomato pasta sauce over the uncooked rissoles before baking.

SERVES 4

Wild venison casserole

Slow-cooking renders less-expensive, tough cuts of meat into rich, comforting food that is ideal for a winter's night. This recipe requires a casserole dish with a heavy lid. It can also be made with beef using blade steak.

2 tablespoons rice bran oil
500g venison, diced
2 medium onions, chopped
1 medium leek, washed well and chopped
4-6 cloves garlic, sliced
½ cup white wine
3 carrots, chopped chunky
1 teaspoon sea salt
1 tablespoon curry powder or 1-2 teaspoons curry paste
440g can chopped tomatoes

Preheat oven to 130°C.

Put 1 tablespoon of oil in a large heavy-based frying pan and sauté venison until browned. Transfer to a casserole dish.

Return pan to the heat and add another tablespoon of oil. Sauté onions until starting to soften. Add leek and garlic and continue to cook for a few more minutes.

Add wine, bring to a boil and reduce slightly. Remove from heat and transfer vegetables and liquid to the casserole dish.

Add the chopped carrot, sea salt, curry powder or paste, and tomatoes to the casserole dish. Mix all ingredients together. Cover casserole dish with a heavy lid.

Cook for 3-4 hours, until the meat is tender. Check every hour or so that there is still sufficient liquid. Serve with rice or mashed potatoes and steamed greens.

Wild deer, goat and rabbit are a good choice for meat-eaters as they are nutritionally, ecologically and ethically superior to farmed animals. Grass-fed organic beef and lamb are good choices, too. Organic meat is still a bit more expensive than non-organic, but it is definitely worth the extra expense for so many reasons.

Braised soy ginger chicken

This quick and richly flavoured semi-roasted chicken dish is a family favourite from Anna's childhood.

1 free-range chicken
500 ml chicken stock
4 tablespoons shoyu
¼ cup molasses
4 tablespoons grated fresh ginger

Preheat oven to 160°C.

Put chicken in a snug-fitting saucepan.

Put remaining ingredients in a screw-top jar and shake to combine. Pour over the chicken and cover.

Place over medium heat and simmer chicken and marinade for 10 minutes. Turn chicken over and simmer for a further 10 minutes.

Remove chicken from the liquid, place in an oven dish and bake for 30 minutes or until, when carved with a knife, juices run clear.

Carve and serve with vegetables or salad. The sauce can be made into a nice gravy if desired.

SERVES 4–6

Greek lamb stew with quinoa

1 tablespoon rice bran oil
4–6 lamb shoulder chops (750g)
½ cup quinoa, rinsed
2 onions, chopped
2 zucchini, sliced
400g can tomatoes
8 cloves garlic, crushed
1 teaspoon sea salt
freshly ground black pepper
2 cups chicken stock
½ cup dry white wine
10–12 black olives
small handful of mint, chopped

Preheat oven to 160°C.

Heat rice bran oil in a heavy-based frying pan and brown lamb chops on both sides. Transfer to a large casserole dish.

Scatter over the quinoa, onion, zucchini, tomatoes, garlic, salt and pepper. Pour on the chicken stock and wine and cover with a tight-fitting lid or foil and cook for 1–1½ hours until lamb is tender.

To serve, sprinkle with olives and mint.

SERVES 4–6

Once the staple of Incan warriors, quinoa is fast becoming a popular gluten-free alternative to rice, bulgur wheat and pasta. It is a valuable food for vegetarians as it supplies complete protein. With its nutty flavour and fluffy texture, it adapts well to sweet and savoury recipes.

Ginger beef salad

In this recipe the beef is cooked rare. Just searing the outside gives the meat a delicious texture and flavour, and leaves certain beneficial enzymes and nutrients intact.

1 teaspoon sesame or coconut oil
300g sirloin beef, cut into 1.5cm-thick steaks
2 tablespoons lemon juice
2 tablespoons olive oil
1 teaspoon toasted sesame oil
2 tablespoons shoyu
2 teaspoons grated fresh ginger
2 tablespoons sesame seeds, toasted
1 red capsicum, deseeded and sliced
200g snow peas or other greens, blanched
250g mung bean sprouts

Put sesame or coconut oil in a hot frying pan. Sear steaks briefly on each side until cooked rare or medium-rare. Transfer to a chopping board and leave for 10 minutes to cool.

Put lemon juice, olive oil, toasted sesame oil, shoyu and ginger in a medium-sized bowl and stir to combine.

Thinly slice the meat. Add to bowl and mix gently with the marinade. Place in refrigerator for at least 30 minutes to marinate.

To serve, transfer meat and marinade into a large bowl. Add sesame seeds, red capsicum, snow peas and mung bean sprouts. Toss gently together and serve in individual bowls.

SERVES 4

Chicken tagine with lemon and olives

This spicy aromatic North African dish is a real crowd-pleaser. Any leftovers will freeze well for another meal.

MARINADE
⅔ cup olive oil
1 tablespoon turmeric
1 tablespoon paprika
1 teaspoon salt
pinch of cayenne pepper
½ teaspoon black pepper

2kg free-range chicken legs, trimmed of excess skin and fat
4 onions, diced
4 cloves garlic, crushed
4 large tomatoes, chopped
2cm piece fresh ginger, grated
juice of 1 lemon
1 bunch fresh coriander, chopped
1 cup green olives
4 preserved lemons (preserved in salt), cut into quarters

☀ Mix marinade ingredients together. Add meat and stir to coat. Refrigerate overnight.

Heat a large frying pan over medium heat. Using tongs, remove chicken pieces from marinade and place in frying pan. (This may need to be done in 2–3 batches.) Sauté chicken on each side until golden, then remove to a large oven dish with a tight-fitting lid and set aside. Preheat oven to 180°C.

Pour remaining marinade into frying pan, add onions and sauté until softened. Add garlic, tomatoes and ginger and simmer, stirring frequently, for 10 minutes over low heat.

Pour sauce over chicken, cover and place in oven. Cook for 20 minutes, then add lemon juice, coriander, olives and preserved lemons.

Continue cooking until olives and lemons are heated through.

Serve with couscous, quinoa or rice.

SERVES 8

Ginger is a warming spice known for improving digestion and circulation. Fresh ginger tea has been found to reduce nausea and cold symptoms. Add fresh grated ginger to oriental soups, curries, marinades, dressings and salads or try mixing it into a tropical fruit salad.

Desserts
&
sweet treats

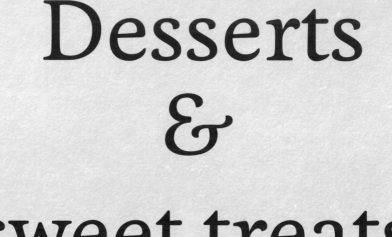

Most Western travellers lose weight when travelling in India. I spent two months there practising yoga and came home many kilos curvier due to my frequent indulgence in the irresistible Indian sweets. These days my sweet tooth is still with me, but I tend to satisfy it with desserts and snacks made from natural sweeteners and unrefined sugars which, surprisingly, are a whole lot more satisfying than most of the sweets we can buy on the run. – ANNA

We are biologically hard-wired to seek out the instantly available energy from carbohydrates, which is why most of us find sweet food irresistible. Such foods were extremely rare and valuable for our pre-industrial ancestors, but in the modern world, sugary foods and drinks are all too common.

Consumed regularly, sweet food causes mood swings and countless health issues, including fatigue, weight gain, lowered immunity, depression, anxiety, bowel problems and yeast overgrowth. Ultimately, the overconsumption of refined sugars contributes to degenerative diseases such as diabetes, heart disease and cancer.

That's why we have repeatedly emphasised the importance of obtaining the bulk of your carbohydrate requirements from whole-food sources. We do recognise, however, that few of us can resist sweet food altogether and so in the following chapter we offer a range of recipes that will satisfy a sweet tooth without feeding unhealthy cravings.

INGREDIENTS THAT MAKE SWEET TREATS HEALTHIER:

❊ Natural sweeteners, eg. dried fruit, honey, stevia and whole cane sugar
❊ Xylitol, a low-calorie sweetener refined from vegetables like maize
❊ Gluten-free flours and spelt flour
❊ Healthy fats and oils, including tahini, butter, coconut oil, rice bran oil
❊ Ground nuts and seeds.

Aside from our hard-wiring, emotional addiction to sweet food is also common. Most of us learn as children and teach our own children that sweet foods are treats, creating an association between sweet food and happy times. As a result, many people consume sweet nibbles and carbohydrates on a regular basis in an attempt to make themselves feel better.

Eating healthy sweet alternatives to white sugary foods is an excellent step. But in excess even healthy treats will cause problems.

OUR PERSONALLY TESTED TIPS FOR CURING A SWEETNESS HABIT:

❊ See a naturopath to find out if you have nutrient deficiencies.
❊ Eat good-quality protein with every meal and reduce your intake of processed grains and flours.
❊ Avoid rigid health-food regimes. An inflexible attitude can magnify cravings.
❊ Let change happen gradually.

A NOTE OF CAUTION: People who suffer from low immunity, *Candida* infections or any serious disease should take care to eat sweet foods made from lower-carbohydrate recipes. Use ground nuts instead of flour, and low-glycaemic sweeteners such as xylitol and stevia.

Persian delights

Plump, moist, fresh Medjool dates are a treat as they are, and this simple pistachio-nut filling makes them an exotic and elegant after-dinner surprise.

¼ cup shelled pistachio nuts
1 teaspoon honey
¼ teaspoon ground cardamom
rind of 1 orange, chopped fine
1 teaspoon rosewater or orange juice
6 fresh Medjool dates

Grind the pistachio nuts in a mortar and pestle almost to a powder, but with a few chunks remaining. Add honey, cardamom, orange zest and rosewater or orange juice. Continue to grind until it is well combined and sticks together.

With a small knife, split each date in half and remove the pit. Stuff each halved date with about 1 teaspoon of pistachio mixture.

Serve on a beautiful platter and decorate with rose petals.

MAKES 12 BITE-SIZED TREATS

Zucchini chocolate no-bake cake

A wonderful use for all those summer zucchini, this cake is raw, vegan and surprisingly delicious! It is more like a dense pudding in consistency and holds its shape well if formed in a cake tin or sculpted into shape.

½ cup walnuts
½ cup hazelnuts
4 tablespoons desiccated coconut
⅓ cup ground sesame seeds
½ cup ground flaxseed
⅓ cup cocoa powder
½ teaspoon ground cinnamon
500g zucchini, chopped
½ cup raisins
¾ cup soft dates, pitted and chopped

Line a 20cm x 20cm cake tin or casserole dish with cling film.

Put walnuts and hazelnuts in a food processor and pulse until still a bit chunky. Transfer ½ cup of these nut chunks into a large bowl and set aside until required. Continue processing remaining nuts until very fine. Add coconut, ground sesame seeds and flaxseed, cocoa and cinnamon and pulse again until well mixed. Add all this to the nuts in the bowl.

Put chopped zucchini in food processor and blend to a pulp. Add raisins and dates. Process again until well mixed.

Add zucchini mixture to nut mixture and knead together.

Spread mixture into prepared tin and press flat. Cover and refrigerate until ready to serve. It is best to leave for at least 2 hours as it will become firmer.

Remove top layer of cling film and turn cake out onto a serving dish.

Spread a layer of *Cashew cream* (see *Fresh fig tart*, page 112) on top. Garnish with flowers or dust with cocoa powder.

SERVES 10

Cinnamon not only has a lovely flavour, it also helps the heart. Research has shown ¼–1½ teaspoons of cinnamon per day can reduce cholesterol, triglycerides and blood glucose. This suggests cinnamon may be beneficial for diabetics and people at risk of heart disease. According to Ayurveda and Chinese medicine, cinnamon is excellent for improving circulation and digestion.

Fresh fig tart

Fresh local figs can only be enjoyed in late summer and autumn as they need to ripen on the tree. Therefore, in our house we call this no-bake dessert Gratitude Pie, as fresh figs remind us to be grateful for the seasons and for locally grown food!

BASE
⅔ cup almonds
½ cup dried figs, chopped
½ cup desiccated coconut
½ cup sesame seeds, ground fine in a
   spice grinder
pinch of sea salt

CASHEW CREAM
1½ cups cashew pieces
2 tablespoons maple syrup or honey
½ cup water

TOPPING
500g fresh figs
1 tablespoon lavender petals (optional)
2 tablespoons honey

☀ Soak almonds and cashew pieces separately overnight.

To make the base, put drained and rinsed almonds and dried figs in a food processor and process until mixture is fine and crumbly.

Add coconut, ground sesame and salt. Process until well combined. (Mixture should stick together when squeezed in your fingers.)

Press into a 20cm flan dish with removable base. Refrigerate until required.

To make the cashew cream, drain and rinse cashew nuts and put in a blender or food processor with maple syrup or honey and water. Blend until fairly smooth.

To assemble tart, spread cashew cream evenly across the base. Trim stalks from figs then slice in half or in chunky wedges. Arrange figs on top of cashew cream.

Mix lavender petals, if using, and honey together with just enough warm water to make a thick syrup. Drizzle syrup over figs. Serve at room temperature.

Leftover tart will keep for several days in the refrigerator. It can also be frozen.

SERVES 12

To make the colourful tart on page 2, use the *Fresh fig tart* recipe but replace the topping with rings of sliced stonefruit and cherries instead of fresh figs.

Spiced tamarillo compote

Tamarillos, also known as tree tomatoes, are a wonderful blend of bitter, sweet and sour. Most people find they need some sweetening. This recipe requires no cooking. The dried fruit is softened with tamarillo juice, creating a sweet, smooth blend of flavours.

6–7 tamarillos (500g)
⅓ cup pitted dates, diced
⅓ cup sultanas
1 teaspoon mixed spice
¼ teaspoon ginger powder
small pinch of sea salt

Using a small sharp knife, cut a cross in the pointy end of each tamarillo. Place in a large bowl and pour on enough boiling water to cover. Leave for 1 minute, then drain and cool. When cool enough to handle, use the small knife again to peel off the skins, which should come away easily.

Cut each tamarillo in half lengthwise, then into 3 or 4 thick slices. Place in a bowl and add remaining ingredients. Mix gently together. Cover bowl and place in the refrigerator. Leave for at least 24 hours before serving.

SERVES 4

Feijoa nut crumble

This warm but raw dessert is a wonderful way to enjoy feijoas, which thrive in a subtropical climate. For an alternative, replace the feijoas with 1½ cups of frozen berries. Heat the crumble just enough to warm through to preserve the fresh flavour of the fruit.

CRUMBLE TOPPING
½ cup sunflower seeds
½ cup dates, pitted and chopped
½ cup walnuts
½ teaspoon ginger powder
pinch of sea salt

FRUIT BASE
500g feijoas
2 cups grated apple
⅓ cup raisins
1 teaspoon ground cinnamon
small pinch of ground cloves
pinch of sea salt

Preheat oven to 120°C.

To make topping, place all ingredients in a food processor and process until mixture has a fine texture. Transfer to a separate bowl until required. (There's no need to wash the food processor before making the fruit base.)

To make fruit base, halve feijoas and scoop out flesh with a spoon into a large bowl. Chop into small chunks.

Put 1 cup of grated apple, raisins, cinnamon, cloves and sea salt in a food processor and process for a few seconds until raisins are mostly puréed.

Transfer mixture to bowl containing feijoas and remaining grated apple. Mix gently with a large spoon.

Place fruit mixture into a shallow ceramic or ovenproof dish and spread out evenly. Sprinkle the crumble mixture on top.

Before serving, heat for 30–40 minutes until warmed through.

Serve with fresh whipped cream or *Soft-serve banana ice-cream* (see page 125).

SERVES 6

Gluten-free coconut orange cake

This low-sugar cake is super-fast to make, although a food processor is essential. You may prefer to use white refined stevia liquid or powder, which doesn't have the strong herbal taste of unprocessed stevia-leaf powder.

2 medium-sized, thin-skinned oranges
6 eggs
½ cup whole cane sugar, xylitol
  or raw sugar
½ teaspoon stevia powder
1⅓ cups desiccated coconut
⅔ cup rice flour
2 teaspoons baking powder

Scrub fruit well. Place in a saucepan over medium heat, cover with water and bring to a boil. Reduce heat to a simmer, cover with a lid and simmer for 1 hour. Change water and simmer for 1 hour further. Drain and, when cool enough to handle, cut fruit in half carefully, and remove any seeds.

Preheat oven to 175°C. Grease and line a medium-sized spring-form cake tin.

Put fruit, skin and all, in a food processor and process to a smooth purée.

Add egg, sweetener and stevia. Process at high speed until thick and lemon-coloured. Add coconut, rice flour and baking powder. Gently pulse to combine. Pour into the prepared tin.

Bake for 45 minutes or until firm and a skewer inserted in the centre comes out clean. Check after 30 minutes and if the top is getting too brown, cover loosely with foil.

SERVES 10–12

Feijoa nut crumble

Coconut cookies

These soft, chewy, gluten-free cookies are simple to make. Brazil nuts, walnuts or almonds can be used instead of cashews and sunflower seeds.

½ cup cashew pieces
½ cup sunflower seeds
1 egg
1 teaspoon vanilla essence
60g melted butter or coconut oil
⅓ cup whole cane sugar, xylitol or raw sugar
½ teaspoon baking soda
pinch of sea salt
1 cup desiccated coconut
2 tablespoons arrowroot

Preheat oven to 180°C. Lightly grease an oven tray.

Put nuts and seeds in a food processor or spice grinder and process until finely ground.

Put egg, vanilla, butter or oil, sweetener, baking soda and salt in a bowl and whisk together. Add ground nuts and seeds, coconut and arrowroot. Mix well.

Working with 1 heaped tablespoon of mixture at a time, press gently to form into a ball and place on prepared tray, leaving about 2cm between each. When all balls are formed, flatten each one slightly so that all are of an even thickness. Bake for 10-15 minutes until brown.

MAKES ABOUT 15 COOKIES

Black rice pudding

Black rice has a delicious creamy texture and exotic, earthy flavour. The rich, white coconut cream topping is a perfect complement to the sweetened rice. This may be eaten warm or cooled and leftovers will keep in the refrigerator for several days.

1 cup glutinous black rice
4 cups water
50g palm sugar or whole cane sugar
pinch of sea salt

COCONUT CREAM TOPPING
400g can coconut cream
pinch of sea salt
1 teaspoon lemon juice
1 tablespoon arrowroot
½ cup mango, pineapple or papaya, diced
  (optional)

Wash and rinse black rice in a sieve. Place in a saucepan with 1 litre of water. Leave to soak for at least 4 hours or overnight.

Place saucepan with drained rice and water over medium heat and bring to a boil. Cover with a lid and turn heat to low. Leave to simmer for about 45 minutes, stirring occasionally, until almost all water is absorbed; the rice should now have a creamy texture – like a pudding.

Add sweetener and sea salt to hot rice. Stir well until sugar has dissolved. Spoon rice into small individual bowls.

To make topping, put coconut cream, salt, lemon juice and arrowroot in a small saucepan over low heat and stir to combine. Slowly bring to a boil. The mixture should thicken slightly.

To serve, pour topping over black rice. Garnish with diced fruit, if using.

SERVES 6-8

Xylitol is a tooth-friendly sweetener because it inhibits the growth of decay-causing bacteria. It is about as sweet as sugar but with two-thirds the food energy and has a very low glycaemic rating. However, it is a highly processed mineral-deficient food that is best used occasionally, in combination with nutrient-rich wholefood ingredients.

Black rice pudding

Pear and cardamom tart

This dessert looks and tastes a treat. It is simple to make, requiring no baking. It is also gluten-, dairy- and refined-sugar-free. Psyllium is not essential to this recipe but it does help the filling to set, making the tart easier to slice and serve.

BASE
⅔ cup almonds
½ cup dates, chopped and pitted
½ cup desiccated coconut
½ cup sesame seeds, finely ground
   in a spice or coffee grinder
1 teaspoon ginger powder
pinch of sea salt

FILLING
1 cup cashew pieces
100g dried apricots
1 large pear, roughly chopped
1 teaspoon ground cardamom
½ teaspoon ground cloves
2 tablespoons psyllium hulls
½ teaspoon sea salt
2–3 pears, sliced thinly

☀ Put almonds for base and cashews for filling in separate bowls and cover with water. Soak overnight. Soak dried apricots overnight in ⅔ cup of water.

Drain almonds and put in a food processor with dates. Process until fine and crumbly.

Add coconut, ground sesame seeds, ginger and salt. Continue to process until well combined. (The mixture should stick together when squeezed in your fingers.)

Press mixture into a 20cm flan dish with a removable base. Refrigerate while making topping. (There's no need to wash food processor before making filling.)

To make filling, drain cashews and put in food processor with the roughly chopped pear, apricots (including most of the soaking liquid), spices, psyllium and salt. Process until smooth.

Remove base from refrigerator and arrange sliced pear over base, reserving a few slices to decorate the top.

Pour cashew and apricot filling over pears and spread evenly.

Decorate tart by carefully arranging reserved pear slices on top.

SERVES 8–10

Strawberry kanten

Traditional kanten jelly is regaining popularity in Japan as the agar agar – a natural setting agent derived from seaweed – moderates the absorption of sugar into the blood and supports bowel health.

3½ cups apple juice
pinch of sea salt
1 teaspoon pure vanilla essence
4½ tablespoons agar agar flakes
3 tablespoons arrowroot
300g mixed fresh or frozen berries

Choose a tray for the jelly, about 20cm x 15 cm. You could also make the jelly in a bowl. If you wish to get your jelly out in one piece, line tray or bowl with cling film.

Pour 3 cups apple juice into a small saucepan. Add salt and vanilla, and sprinkle on agar agar flakes. Heat slowly until agar agar dissolves. Gradually bring to a boil, turn down heat and simmer for 5 minutes.

Mix arrowroot powder in remaining apple juice until dissolved. Pour this slowly into the saucepan, whisking continuously. Keep whisking until whole mixture thickens and returns to the boil.

Place berries in prepared tray or bowl. Carefully pour on the kanten jelly, taking care to keep the berries evenly distributed. Refrigerate until cool and set.

When set, slice into squares, or scoop out with a spoon. Serve with *Cashew cream* (see *Fresh fig tart*, page 112) or yoghurt.

SERVES 6

Pear and cardamon tart

Sunny banana truffles

¾ cup sunflower seeds
½ cup rolled oats
½ large ripe banana
¼ cup dried coconut
100g dried figs (about 6 figs)
1 teaspoon ginger powder
pinch of sea salt
extra desiccated coconut, or carob or
   sesame seeds

Put sunflower seeds and rolled oats in a food processor. Blend on high speed until they are the texture of coarse breadcrumbs. Add remaining ingredients and blend briefly until combined.

Form into little balls. Roll each ball in coconut, carob or sesame seeds.

MAKES ABOUT 10 SNACK-SIZED BALLS

Cashew apricot bliss balls

1½ cups cashew pieces
1½ cups dried apricots, roughly chopped
½ cup desiccated coconut
½ teaspoon ginger powder
¼ teaspoon ground cardamom
pinch of sea salt
zest of 1 orange
extra desiccated coconut, or carob or
   sesame seeds

Put all ingredients in a food processor and process for several minutes until mixture can be pressed into a ball. If necessary, add a little water to help mixture combine. (Start with just 1 teaspoon of water.)

Form into little balls. Roll each ball in coconut, carob or sesame seeds.

MAKES ABOUT 16 SNACK-SIZED BALLS

Chai spice and prune cake

2 black tea bags
1 cup boiling water
250g pitted prunes, halved
¼ cup (5 tablespoons) honey
300g spelt flour
1 teaspoon baking soda
1 teaspoon baking powder
2 teaspoons ground cinnamon
1 teaspoon mixed spice
½ teaspoon ground cardamom
1 teaspoon ginger powder
½ teaspoon sea salt
125g butter, melted or ½ cup rice bran oil
2 free-range eggs
2 medium-sized apples (300g), cored and grated

Preheat oven to 180°C. Grease and flour a 32cm round cake tin and line base with baking paper.

Put tea bags in a small saucepan and pour on boiling water. After 5 minutes remove teabags and put saucepan over medium heat. Add prunes and bring to a gentle boil. Simmer for 5 minutes to soften prunes. Turn heat off, add honey and stir to dissolve. Set aside to cool slightly.

Sift spelt flour, baking soda, baking powder, spices and sea salt into a bowl. Mix well.

Put butter or oil and eggs in another large bowl and whisk together. Add grated apple and the warm prune and tea mixture. Mix wet ingredients well. Add dry ingredients. Gently stir together until just combined.

Pour into prepared tin and bake for 30–40 minutes until firm to touch in the centre.

Serve warm or cold with a dollop of thick natural yoghurt or fresh whipped cream.

SERVES 10–12

Soft-serve banana ice-cream

These banana-based ice-creams have a soft, creamy consistency and need to be consumed immediately, but that is seldom a problem! Dairy-free and without added sugar, they are perfect for people with dietary restrictions.

VANILLA BANANA ICE-CREAM
3 bananas
⅓ cup cashew pieces
150ml coconut cream, rice milk or soy milk
1 teaspoon pure vanilla essence

CHOCOLATE BANANA ICE-CREAM
3 bananas
⅓ cup cashew pieces
150ml coconut cream, rice milk or soy milk
3 tablespoons cocoa powder or carob
1 teaspoon ginger powder
½ teaspoon pure vanilla essence

RASPBERRY BANANA ICE-CREAM
3 bananas
⅓ cup cashew pieces
150ml coconut cream, rice milk or soy milk
½ cup frozen raspberries

☀ Prepare bananas at least 8 hours in advance. Chop bananas into bite-sized pieces and freeze. Soak cashew pieces overnight and drain.

Put all ingredients except bananas in a food processor and process until well puréed. With the food processor still running, gradually add frozen banana pieces.

Serve immediately, as it goes very hard when frozen.

EACH RECIPE SERVES 4

Piña colada ice-cream

When we have surplus fruit we chop it into small pieces and freeze it ready to make this delicious frozen dessert. The ice-cream will go completely solid if placed back in the freezer, so only make as much as you need.

½ pineapple
½ fresh banana
¼ cup coconut cream

Prepare pineapple at least 8 hours in advance. Remove skin and tough core, chop flesh into bite-sized pieces and freeze.

Put banana and coconut cream in a food processor or strong blender. Blend until smooth.

With the food processor still running, gradually add frozen pineapple pieces, then blend until mixture is smooth.

Spoon into 4 small bowls and eat immediately.

SERVES 4

For some, food is merely a fuel, used to top up energy levels when required. For others, food and emotions are bound up in a complex relationship of pleasure and guilt. Judging yourself for 'being naughty' in relation to food or worrying about getting fat when eating is more damaging to your health than the occasional piece of cake! If you do struggle with food issues, we recommend you seek help from an experienced therapist, a 12-step programme, or undertake an EFT (Emotional Freedom Technique) course.

Soft-serve banana ice-cream

Chocolate mint squares

Here's our delicious wheat-, dairy- and sugar-free alternative to chocolate fudge. Serve these squares with fresh strawberries, all piled up together for dramatic effect.

½ cup almonds
½ cup sesame seeds
⅓ cup desiccated coconut
⅓ cup cocoa powder
8 large dried figs (150g), sliced
½ cup dates, pitted and chopped
2 drops pure peppermint essence
2 tablespoons water

☀ Soak almonds in water overnight, then drain.

Line a 10cm x 20cm loaf tin with cling film.

Grind sesame seeds in a spice grinder or coffee mill until fine. (Do this in 2-3 batches if necessary.)

Put all ingredients in a food processor and process on high speed until mixture has a fine, crumbly texture. Squeeze some of the mixture in your fingers – it should be just moist enough to hold together. Add a little bit more water if necessary.

Press mixture into the bottom of prepared loaf tin and refrigerate for 30 minutes until firm.

To serve, remove from tin and slice into squares.

MAKES ABOUT 18 SQUARES

Beetroot chocolate cake

This may sound like an odd combination for a cake, but most people are amazed when they try it. The beetroot keeps the cake moist, just as carrots do in a carrot cake. What a great way to eat vegetables, nuts and seeds!

¼ cup flaxseed
⅓ cup almonds
⅓ cup sunflower seeds
300g beetroot, trimmed and scrubbed
¾ cup rice bran oil, grapeseed oil or melted butter
1 cup whole cane sugar or brown sugar
2 free-range eggs
½ teaspoon pure vanilla essence
1 cup spelt flour
2 teaspoons baking powder
½ cup cocoa

Preheat oven to 180°C. Grease and flour a 23cm round cake tin.

Grind flaxseed fine in a spice grinder or mortar and pestle. Transfer to a large bowl.

In a food processor, grind almonds and sunflower seeds as fine as possible using the S blade. Add to the flaxseed.

Grate beetroot using the fine grating attachment of a food processor. Add to nuts and seeds.

Fit blending blade to food processor. Place oil, sugar, eggs and vanilla into food processor. Blend on high for a couple of minutes. Transfer to a large bowl. Sift flour, baking powder, and cocoa onto the wet mix. Add grated beetroot, ground nuts and seeds. Stir everything together until just combined. (The mixing can be completed in the food processor if it is large enough.)

Pour into prepared tin and bake for 35-40 minutes until an inserted skewer comes out clean.

SERVES 8–12

We make *Beetroot chocolate cake* in a food processor. There's a bit of juggling with the blending and grating attachments, but there's no need to wash out the processor bowl between any of these steps.

Avocado chocolate mousse

This surprisingly rich, smooth mousse is dairy-free. Avocado is the magic ingredient – its healthy oils create a luscious creamy texture. It keeps well in the refrigerator for more than 10 days – if you can resist dipping into it!

½ cup dehydrated sugar cane juice or honey
½ cup water
2 medium-sized avocados (300g flesh)
1 teaspoon pure vanilla essence
¼ teaspoon ground cinnamon
½ cup good quality cocoa powder
juice of ½ small lemon

Put all ingredients in a food processor and process to combine.

Refrigerate until required.

SERVES 8

Apricot muesli bar

Many store-bought muesli bars contain high levels of sugar, hydrogenated oils and preservatives. Some also contain artificial colouring. This low-glycaemic recipe is a much healthier (and tastier) alternative. Many thanks to Nicola Galloway, author, nutrition consultant and chef, for providing the original inspiration behind the recipe.

200g apricots, chopped
1 cup fruit juice
2 eggs
75g butter, melted
2 cups fine rolled oats
1 cup desiccated coconut
⅓ cup wholemeal spelt flour
½ teaspoon ground cinnamon
½ teaspoon baking powder
pinch of sea salt

Preheat oven to 180°C. Grease and line a 15cm x 25cm slice tin.

Put chopped apricots in a bowl with the fruit juice.

Whisk together eggs and butter. Add to fruit mixture.

Combine dry ingredients in a separate bowl. Add wet ingredients and mix until well combined.

Press into prepared tin and bake for 20–25 minutes until firm and starting to colour.

Slice when cool and store in an airtight container.

MAKES ABOUT 15 BARS

Avocado chocolate mousse

Drinks

❁✾✾✾✾✾✾✾✾✾❁

Once while hiking a remote track in the hills behind Nelson, we rested beside a stream before beginning a long steep climb. Anna suggested we fill our water bottles but I resisted, sure we'd pass plenty of other streams and adamant we wouldn't want the extra weight. Many hours later, hot, thirsty and anxious, we were so relieved to find a small pond. Anna graciously forgave me. I have since learned to be more cautious. – **ROGER**

Just like a garden, we also need regular watering to be at our best! Limiting your fluid intake can lead to fatigue, dry skin, headaches and constipation. When we become dehydrated the first thing to suffer is our clarity of thought.

WATER
Drinking sufficient water is even more important than eating. With plenty of water and no food, people can survive for at least 30 days. However, without water you could die within five days.

How much water do you need? You can get 20-40 per cent of your required daily fluids from eating fresh fruit and vegetables. The remainder must come from drinking and water is always the best choice to quench a thirst. Most experts agree that approximately eight glasses of water per day is sufficient to maintain proper hydration. Begin your day with a glass of water because you lose a lot of water during the night due to respiration and metabolic processes.

To carry water for drinking, we recommend using bottles made of stainless steel, strong glass with a padded carrier case or stable plastic. Look for plastic bottles marked with recycling number 1. Avoid PVC (marked with a number 3) and polycarbonate (marked with a number 7). Never leave plastic water bottles in a car - heat degrades plastic which can cause chemicals to leach into the water.

SOFT DRINKS

Fizzy drinks, energy drinks and fruit-flavoured drinks contain plenty of sugary energy and have minimal nutritional value. Studies clearly show a strong link between soft-drink consumption and childhood health issues, such as obesity, tooth decay, caffeine dependence and weak bones, indicating that soft drinks are completely unsuitable for children.

FRUIT JUICE

Fruit juice is often promoted as a healthy alternative to sugary drinks. Pure fruit juice is a relatively natural product and contains none of the additives found in soft drinks. However, it is high in fructose (fruit sugar) and can cause the same extreme response in blood-sugar and insulin levels as sucrose (white sugar). If you drink fruit juice in any quantity it is best to drink it diluted with water. This is especially important for young children.

CAFFEINE

A fit, healthy person can safely enjoy one daily coffee. However, regularly drinking several cups a day can cause a range of problems including difficulty losing weight, anaemia and sleep problems. Anyone with compromised physical or mental health should avoid caffeine completely. Both black and green teas contain caffeine too – although many varieties of tea also have some health benefits. There are many satisfying substitutes for caffeinated drinks, such as herbal teas and dandelion root coffee.

ALCOHOL

One or two glasses of alcohol per day has some positive heart-health benefits. Red wine is known to be a healthier choice due to antioxidant phenolic compounds. However, alcohol is an addictive substance that contributes to widespread health issues and social distress. Try going without alcohol for several days – withdrawal symptoms or cravings are a sure sign of addiction.

MILK

Our experience and research has led us to believe that pasteurised and homogenised milk does not contribute to optimum health. However, the process of fermenting milk into yoghurt and other cultures can reduce the lactose content by 30-40 per cent, which is why people who have difficulty digesting milk may feel fine after eating yoghurt.

Here is our list of the most easily digested and nourishing milks to drink or use in cooking:

❊ Fresh raw goat's and cow's milk
❊ Homemade nut and seed milk
❊ Packaged almond milk, rice milk and oat milk
❊ Whole (unhomogenised) cow's milk.

Mango cardamom lassi

This is an exotic, healthy treat – it's refreshing, nourishing and balancing. It may be enjoyed at breakfast, as a snack, or as a dessert, and is the perfect way to finish a curry meal.

Acidophilus yoghurt contains probiotics that help create healthy intestines.

1 fresh ripe mango, peeled and stone removed
1½ cups unsweetened acidophilus yoghurt
2 teaspoons honey
pinch of sea salt
¼ teaspoon ground cardamom

Put all ingredients in a blender and blend until smooth and creamy.

Pour into 2 glasses and serve immediately.

SERVES 2

Probiotics are supplements of beneficial intestinal bacteria. Within your intestine are about 2 kilograms of bacteria! Probiotics assist the body to keep a balanced ecology of gut flora. When things get out of balance, due to things like overeating sugary foods or taking antibiotics, *Candida* infections and bowel problems can manifest themselves. Probiotics come from eating non-digestible foods like fibre. They help good bacteria thrive and stay healthy. Eating a diet rich in wholefoods ensures we get plenty of probiotics.

Chocolate almond smoothie

1 banana, peeled and chopped
1½ tablespoons cocoa powder
⅓ cup almonds, soaked overnight, drained and
  rinsed ☀
1 tablespoon honey
½ teaspoon pure vanilla essence
1 cup water

Put all ingredients in a blender and blend until smooth and creamy.

Pour into 2 glasses and serve immediately.

SERVES 2

Raspberry avocado smoothie

1 banana, peeled and chopped
1 small avocado, peeled and stone removed
1 cup frozen raspberries
1 tablespoon honey
1 cup water
small pinch of sea salt

Put all the ingredients in a blender and blend until smooth and creamy.

Pour into 2 glasses and serve immediately.

SERVES 2

Make *Raspberry cream* by omitting the water from the *Raspberry avocado smoothie*. In this thicker form, it can be used as an alternative to yoghurt for breakfast or with sliced fresh fruit for dipping.

Pineapple mint cocktail

For a taste of summer, pineapple is hard to beat.

½ pineapple
10 medium-sized mint leaves
small piece of fresh ginger, sliced or grated
pinch of sea salt
1 cup water
honey (optional)

Peel pineapple and remove any tough spikes, hollows or bumps. Remove core and chop flesh into chunks.

Put all ingredients except honey in a blender and blend until smooth.

Taste and add honey if required.

Serve immediately or refrigerate until ready to serve.

SERVES 4

Iced berry tea

Get the flavour of summer berries all year round with this refreshing berry tea.

2 cups water
3 berry-flavoured herbal tea bags
6 slices fresh ginger
½ orange, sliced
4 tablespoons honey
500ml dark grape juice, chilled
1 litre sparkling or still water, chilled

Combine 2 cups water, teabags, ginger, orange slices and honey in a large saucepan on medium heat and slowly bring to a boil. Simmer for 10 minutes. Leave to cool for 30 minutes then chill in the refrigerator.

When ready to serve, mix this concentrate with chilled grape juice and chilled sparkling or still water.

To serve, pour over ice in individual glasses.

SERVES 6

Lemon iced tea

In the hottest days of summer take time to relax and sip on a glass of iced tea.

3 cups boiling water
3 black tea bags
2 tablespoons honey
juice of 2 lemons
lots of ice cubes
lemon slices

Pour water onto the tea bags. Leave tea to steep for about 5 minutes. Discard tea bags.

Stir honey into hot tea.

Pour lemon juice into 4 glasses.

Three-quarters fill each glass with ice.

Pour tea over ice in each glass.

Do not squeeze out the tea bags as these last traces can be very bitter. Stir well. Garnish with slices of lemon.

SERVES 4

Add fresh mint or lavender flowers to each glass along with the ice, but before pouring the tea.

Left: Iced berry tea
Overleaf left: Lemon iced tea. Overleaf right: Sweet spiced tea

Sparkly fruit punch

The zesty flavour of fresh fruit makes this punch a real crowd-pleaser. It is also easy to multiply the recipe for a large party.

2–3 oranges (250g), peeled and flesh
  roughly chopped
1 litre apple or pear juice
500ml sparkling mineral water
1 cup frozen mixed berries
handful of fresh mint leaves

Blend orange flesh with 1 cup of fruit juice.

In a large bowl, mix blended orange and remaining fruit juice and all other ingredients.

MAKES 8 GLASSES

Ginger rooibos tea

Rooibos (red bush) tea from South Africa has a robust satisfying flavour. It is also caffeine- and tannin-free. In winter, try adding fresh ginger for a warming drink with extra zing.

3 rooibos tea bags
fresh ginger slices
1.5 litres cold water

Put all the ingredients in a saucepan over medium heat and bring slowly to a boil. Simmer for 5 minutes. Alternatively, use a coffee plunger and simply leave to steep for 5 minutes.

Strain and serve immediately.

MAKES 6 CUPS

Sweet spiced tea

Share this wonderful warming drink with friends on special winter occasions. Omit any of the spices that are not easy to obtain – it will still be delicious.

2 liquorice tea bags
½ teaspoon fennel seed
½ teaspoon aniseed
½ teaspoon star anise
1 teaspoon cardamom pods
8 dried dates
fresh ginger slices
2 fresh orange slices
1.5 litres cold water
small pinch of sea salt

Put all ingredients in a saucepan over medium heat and gradually bring to a boil. Turn heat down and simmer for about 15 minutes.

Strain and serve immediately.

MAKES 6 CUPS

Glossary

ARAME
This Japanese sea vegetable has a fine, firm texture with a mild flavour that can enhance many salads and soups. Soak for 30 minutes before use.

BEE POLLEN
Bee pollen is flower pollen that is collected from bees' bodies as they enter a hive. Pollen is a nourishing food, containing essential amino acids and many vitamins and minerals.

BLACK RICE
A deep purple when cooked, black rice has a nutty taste and soft texture, and is high in iron and other nutrients. Available from Asian food stores.

BOK CHOY
A dark green variety of the mustard family, it comprises bunches of firm-textured leaves with thick, crunchy white stems.

BUCKWHEAT
This gluten-free triangular-shaped seed is often referred to as a grain, but is, more accurately, a small dried fruit. Buckwheat is native to Central Asia and a significant food in Russia. It is traditionally cooked whole or ground into a flour, but it can be sprouted and eaten raw.

CAROB
The carob tree is native to the Mediterranean. The dried ground flesh of the pod has a flavour similar to sweetened cocoa. It contains no caffeine and is often used as a non-allergenic cocoa substitute.

CHINESE FIVE-SPICE
A balanced mixture of ground spices designed to combine the five flavours of Chinese cooking. A typical mix includes cinnamon, black pepper, cloves, fennel seed and star anise.

CHLORELLA
A dark-green single-celled freshwater algae, chlorella is a great source of protein and micronutrients. It is a valuable detoxification aid and is excellent mixed with a little juice or in a smoothie.

COCONUT OIL
Coconut oil is very stable at higher cooking temperatures and rarely goes rancid. The saturated fat in coconut oil is in a form that is easy to assimilate and does not have the same adverse effect as the saturated fat in animal products. It is anti-bacterial and can speed up the metabolism.

DAIKON
The literal translation of daikon is 'large root'. It is a long, fat, white root-vegetable with crisp texture and mild radish flavour; delicious grated in salads and wraps. It is also known as Chinese radish.

DEHYDRATED SUGAR CANE JUICE
The texture, golden colour and caramel flavour lend well to baking. It retains minerals that are stripped away to make white sugar. Rapadura is the Portuguese word for unrefined dehydrated sugar cane juice and a brand that we recommend.

FEIJOA
A relative of the guava, feijoa is an egg-shaped fruit with a green skin and a pulpy, deliciously aromatic flesh. Originally from the Brazilian highlands, this small tree grows well in a subtropical climate.

FLAXSEED
Consumed as an oil or as freshly ground seed, flaxseed is becoming popular as a nutritional supplement, mainly for its omega-3 content. Sometimes called linseed, it can be ground and used in baking or pancakes to replace eggs.

GLUTEN
A protein found in some grains, including wheat, rye and barley. Gluten gives wheat dough its elasticity. An allergy to gluten causes the digestive disorder known as coeliac disease. Gluten may also be found in many additives to processed food.

HIJIKI
This Japanese sea vegetable is ink-black in colour with a firm texture and strong taste of the sea. It brings a dramatic dimension to salads.

KALE
A member of the brassica family, kale has dark-green leaves that do not form a head. It is the closest form of cultivated brassica to wild cabbage. It is very hardy, pest-resistant, easy to grow and, possibly, has even more nutritional benefits than broccoli.

KARENGO
This sea vegetable, harvested in the South Island of New Zealand, is very closely related to Japanese nori. It is purple and becomes soft and slimy when soaked.

KOMBU
This wide flat seaweed is a good source of calcium, iron, protein, and vitamins A, B1 and B2. We add it to cooking beans to bring out the flavour and increase digestibility. It is also delicious soaked and cooked in miso soup but needs to be removed and sliced, then added back before serving.

KUMARA
The Maori word for New Zealand sweet potato, kumara can be used in the same way as the American sweet potato or yam.

MEDJOOL DATES
Originally from Morocco, these large, succulent dates are grown in the USA and are often labelled California dates.

MILLET
A mineral-rich gluten-free grain, small and round in shape. Millet is a staple food in Africa.

MISO

Fermented soya bean paste. Some varieties are made with added grains. Although a cooked product, miso is fermented for months or years and is alive with healthy enzymes.

MIZUNA

This mild-tasting leafy Chinese green, a member of the mustard family, has feathery leaves with a white stem.

NORI

A variety of seaweed from Far-East Asia most commonly seen in its processed form, as sheets for making rolled sushi.

POMEGRANATE MOLASSES

Made from concentrated pomegranate juice, this dark-brown liquid has a versatile sweet-and-sour flavour. It can be found at Mediterranean specialty stores.

PSYLLIUM HULLS

Psyllium is a native Mediterranean plant. The seed hulls are most commonly used as a bulking and lubrication aid for the digestive system. When moistened, psyllium hulls expand, becoming jelly-like, and as such make an excellent thickener in some desserts.

PUHA

A nutrient-rich leaf vegetable also known as sow thistle which, when cooked, tastes similar to chard.

RAW HONEY

In its raw form, honey contains many valuable enzymes, vitamins, minerals and other factors. Most commercial honeys are pasteurised to guarantee long storage; however, the processing destroys many of the micronutrients. Buy raw honey from the farm gate or at farmers' markets.

QUINOA

Often called a grain, this is a small, round white fruit of the goosefoot plant, a native to the Andes. It can be eaten sprouted, ground to be used as a flour or cooked in a similar way to rice. It is very high in protein.

SEA SALT

Salt produced simply by the evaporation of sea water contains a broad range of minerals and has a more rounded, complex taste than refined salt. Some of the better varieties of sea salt actually have a dirty-grey appearance.

SHOYU

Shoyu is the Japanese word for 'soy sauce' and is now used in the West to distinguish good-quality fermented soy sauce from inferior unfermented versions.

SPELT

A highly nutritious and ancient grain from the wheat family, spelt can replace standard wheat flour in baked goods, white sauces and pastas.

SPIRULINA

This dehydrated powder made from freshwater algae is one of the richest known sources of complete protein. It is also an excellent source of vitamins, minerals, anti-oxidants, chlorophyll and essential fats.

STEVIA

A sweetener derived from a tropical plant native to South America, stevia contains compounds which are 250–300 times sweeter than table sugar. However, it does not significantly alter blood glucose, and so can be safely consumed by diabetics.

TAHINI

Ground sesame seed paste, and a traditional Middle-Eastern ingredient, tahini is a good alternative to butter and peanut butter. Unhulled tahini is darker and a useful source of calcium and other minerals.

TAMARI

This Japanese word describes the rich liquid that leaches out of miso. In the West, however, the term usually refers to wheat-free fermented shoyu.

TAMARIND PASTE

From the South-East Asian tamarind tree, this sticky pulp surrounds the seeds inside the fruit pods. It has a sweet and sour taste. Available in Asian food stores either as a block (in which case you need to check there are no seeds in it) or as a concentrated liquid (easy to use but has been processed).

TEMPEH

A food made from fermented soya beans. Originally from Indonesia, tempeh has a richer heavier texture and flavour than tofu.

UMEBOSHI VINEGAR

This sour, salty liquid is derived from making Japanese pickled plums (umeboshi paste) and is perfect in Asian-style salad dressings. The paste imparts a tangy, salty flavour to many dishes. Lovely on warm brown rice, in sushi rolls or with tahini on toast.

WAKAME

This Japanese sea vegetable is most often used in traditional miso soup. It has silky firm-textured fronds with a mild flavour. Usually sold as 'fueru wakame', cut into small pieces that only need to be soaked, sometimes it may be found whole in a dried form with the tough stems intact – in which case it needs to be soaked, then de-stemmed and chopped.

XYLITOL

This non-nutritive tooth-friendly sweetener has minimal impact on blood sugar. Xylitol is found in many fruits and vegetables. Originally derived from birch trees, today it is most commonly made from maize.

Recipe index *(numbers in bold indicate recipe photographs)*